Tony Birks

LUCIE RIE

Alphabooks
A & C Black · London

Copyright © 1987 Tony Birks

First published 1987 by
Alphabooks Ltd, Sherborne, Dorset
A subsidiary of
A & C Black plc
35 Bedford Row, London WC1

Design by Albert Clamp in association with the author.

ISBN 0 906670 46 2

British Library Cataloguing in Publication Data
Birks, Tony
   Lucie Rie.
   1. Rie, Lucie   2. Women potters — England
   — Biography
   I. Title
   738'.092'4   NK4210.R5

ISBN 0–906670–46–2

Printed by Jolly & Barber Ltd, Rugby, Warwickshire

Contents

Acknowledgements

Lucie Rie's life encompasses all of the twentieth century. Many of her friends and contemporaries have died, a familiar enough experience for octogenarians, but her friendships endure, and many potters and others have known her for as long as England has been her home. To all her friends she is known simply as Lucie, and throughout the text I refer to her by her Christian name, for the alternatives: 'Mrs Rie', 'Ms Rie', or worse, 'Rie', seem awkward and inappropriate.

Her closest friend Hans Coper died in 1981 and I am sorry to have missed the opportunity of talking to him about his long friendship with her, but many other people close to Lucie have assisted in the preparation of this book. Her numerous women friends have given me much help and information, yet it is true that a succession of major male influences on her have, if not greatly affecting her work, conditioned her thinking and have mattered most in her life. Dr Max Mayer, whom she met as recently as 1962, is probably the person on whom she now most relies, and I too have found his help invaluable.

As in the case of my biography of Hans Coper, I was approached by Sir Robert and Lady Sainsbury with an offer of help to make sure that the book would be produced in a style worthy of its subject, and to them and to many other people I am very grateful. Jane Coper's painstaking photographs speak for themselves. It is always a pleasure to work with her. I know no-one who has more sympathy with Lucie Rie's pots or could cope better with the difficult task of showing a three-dimensional object in a single shot.

T.B.
Somerset, 1987

Porcelain vase, 195 mm, manganese glaze, 1953. Coll. Dora Raeburn.

Introduction: subtlety and simplicity

Lucie Rie's artistic achievement is closely related to the encouragement and the personal inspiration provided by a series of men. As Lucie herself says, 'I am man-made.' In her slow and purposeful rise from youthful promise in post-Secession Vienna to world renown, it is ironic that the death of fellow potter Hans Coper, her greatest inspiration and friend, in 1981, should have placed Lucie Rie in an unassailable position as the world's greatest living potter: it seems clear that as an active artist, whose mastery has not diminished and who never ceases to work, this will remain the case for the rest of her life.

There will always be disputes about the borderline between pottery and sculpture, and several of the most prominent workers in ceramics, especially those of the United States, lie uneasily across this ever-shifting divide. This is not their fault, nor does it diminish their work. Sculpture at its best rises so far above craft as to make the comparison pointless, yet 'straightforward' pottery can rise to great heights, and this is the case with the work of Lucie Rie. Her work never extends beyond pottery; it is not pretentious but it has very special qualities. The purpose of this book is not to describe her work piece by piece, but to describe the life and background of the elusive person who is responsible for it, and perhaps to help unravel the real mystery of why it is so good.

Simple, yet infinitely subtle and complex, Lucie Rie pots approach excellence not by refinement to an ever purer shape: it is by their sturdiness *and* their frailty: a combination of opposites, economy and luxuriance, lightness and dark. Perhaps above all, it is their correct-ness *and* fallibility – the inimitable Lucie Rie 'quiver' – which holds the attention of observers of her work. As a person, she shows the same combination of op-posites. Her diminutive size and apparent frailty belie her determination, her capacity for work and, in her younger days, her physical delight in testing her body to its limits. She turned her smallness and lightness to advantage when this was possible in sport, just as she maximizes the sculptural advantages of centrifugal tendencies of clay on the wheel, which other potters try to fight. In the words of an old friend, the architect John Pike, 'she is quite an engineer.' After sixty-five years of familiarity with the potter's wheel, she can afford to take liberties and risks – using a combination of experience and intuition – and in this her work mirrors her life.

Lucie and her brother Paul photographed in their Vienna home.

1 Vienna and Eisenstadt

'The fortunate years for Vienna' is how the catalogue of the Great Viennese Exhibition of 1986 described the period into which Lucie Rie was born, was educated, grew up, and was trained. This cultural melting-pot, which embraced Mahler, Gropius, Wittgenstein and Freud, as well as a host of revolutionary painters, certainly surrounded her. Born in 1902 she was the third child of Benjamin and Gisela Gomperz. Father Gomperz was a man of medicine – an ear, nose and throat specialist with a good practice in the centre of Vienna – and his wife was the seventh daughter of the redoubtable Ignaz Wolf from Eisenstadt, head of a Jewish family of great wealth and influence.

The family lived in Elizabethstrasse, and Professor Gomperz conducted his practice from the house. At the turn of the century in Vienna, medical methods for testing for deafness were fairly basic. He would take his patients into a long corridor in the house, face them one way and whisper from the other end of the corridor. If they heard, he would face them the other way, and test the other ear. But the Gomperz household was an enlightened one and prosperous enough to take holidays in seaside resorts on the English Channel coast at a time when long-distance travel had to be by train and coach-and-horses. When decisions had to be taken about Lucie's education, a private tutor, Joseph Hellman, was engaged for those years which would correspond to primary schooling. A big, daunting but kindly man, he was a socialist, and Lucie remembers that after lessons he would patiently talk to Gisela Gomperz about his politics, and he found that she shared his views.

It is quite characteristic of city children that their most vivid recollections are of events remembered from visits to the country, and the family tie which attached Lucie's mother to Eisenstadt took the children there regularly and often. In those days a two-hour journey from Vienna, Eisenstadt is best known as the home of

The family house at Eisenstadt: Lucie's Uncle Sandor installed the railings.

Joseph Haydn, because of his association with the Esterhazy family. It was said that whatever in Eisenstadt did not belong to the Esterhazys belonged to the family Wolf, although the wealth that was in evidence to

9

Lucie's grandmother, Hermine Wolf, by the summerhouse at Eisenstadt.

young Lucie's eyes was rather down to earth, and based on winemaking. Her grandmother, Hermine, was a matriarchal figure of whom most of the numerous grandchildren were in awe. The large and beautiful house of the Wolf family had a cool courtyard, with a central pear tree, and here the grandchildren would come to kiss Grandmother's hand.

Lucie in Velden in 1905

Left: Benjamin Gomperz with his mother-in-law. Below: Lucie, with her mother Gisela Gomperz, in Velden in 1908.

There were several Jewish families in Eisenstadt, and the Jewish quarter, with the word 'ghetto' carved into the arch at its entrance, is today a preserved area, with at its centre the former home of the Wolfs. 'Ghetto' in Eisenstadt did not have any implications of constraint on liberty. The iron chains – still in position – which were stretched across the road at both ends of the ghetto were not to keep people apart: they were to stop traffic – carts and cars – disturbing the Jewish peace on the Sabbath day.

Viennese-born Lucie, who must have been used to city streets and traffic, spent her formative years with a great love of country life, and of the country pursuits of the languid and privileged class – sports of all kinds. The energy of the intelligent offspring of this fortunate family was directed towards physical excellence, sometimes of an esoteric or even rather foolish kind – there is a story of a cousin who would eat cherries and learned to spit the stones out precisely on to plates laid out along the long family table as he passed.

The coach and horses would collect Gomperz youngsters from the Vienna train at the station, and whisk them off across Eisenstadt for weekends of walking and riding. The youngsters played tennis on the tennisplatz, while Grandmother Wolf was driven out each day to the summerhouse, where she would

For Lucie, the Brunnerwiese meadow above Eisenstadt was a magical place – a field of flowers and summer pleasures.

write her letters. Sometimes weekends were spent just lying about, especially on the Brunnerwiese meadow above Eisenstadt, where the Wolfs' land ended and the Esterhazy estates began. The photographs of this time, with bodies in the long grass, are rather comic to our eyes, but they are evocative of summer warmth and physical well-being. Other contemporary photographs of Eisenstadt show workers from the winery with barrels and a cart, a world apart. The family kept copious records of events and holidays, from which the accompanying photographs are drawn, but there was to be a lengthy interruption to the pattern of life with the coming of the First World War.

Although obscured by later memories of a much more traumatic time of Jewish persecution, this Great War broke out when Lucie was twelve years old and brought relative hardship to the family, with food shortages and fewer servants. Visits to the country were less frequent and activity in Vienna was curtailed by the hostilities. Lucie was sent to the Gymnasium, a private school where she was supposed to get a fairly gentle secondary education, although she remembers it as hard. In preparation for what she calls being a 'higher daughter', she had extra English lessons, and reluctantly learned the piano with the bony-fingered Fraulein Wassely. She did not have close contact with the war, but she remembers carrying apricots she had gathered herself in baskets to the railway station in

In 1915 prisoners of war from Serbia joined the workforce at the Eisenstadt winery.

In 1916, brother Teddy in military costume salutes his sister at Marienbad.

Eisenstadt to give to the departing soldiers, and she was encouraged in this by her brother Paul. He himself grew vegetables and sold them to raise money for the needy. The Ries' elder son Teddy was a lieutenant in the Austrian army. Their second son Paul was not a sturdy young man, and had no inclination to be a soldier. Nevertheless, he signed up when he was nineteen to avoid being called a 'Jewish coward', and went to the front in Italy to join his cousin Franz. Two weeks later in the battle of Laporetto he was shot in the mouth, and died some hours later. The young Lucie, fifteen, heard the devastating news on her return from a party, and vowed never to enjoy herself again. This artistic, delightful favourite brother had been instrumental in getting Lucie a special tutor for drawing, and was anxious to persuade her rather conventional medical father that her artistic talents needed developing: that she should be properly trained as an artist. But it was another four years before she was to enter art school.

In Lucie's teenage years, one man stands out. Alexander Wolf, 'Uncle Sandor', Lucie's mother's brother, was in charge of the family's affairs in Eisenstadt. The bachelor uncle was a man of immense and eclectic intellectual vision; a collector, a world traveller, a man who fell in love again and again but never managed to persuade his possessive mother that he should marry.

By the time that Lucie was a teenager, Uncle Sandor was the most prominent businessman in the town, but he spent part of the winter in Vienna, and part travelling the world, adding to his collection of artefacts, both Jewish and non-Jewish. Sandor was never happy unless he was in the company of young women, and it was his delight to take Lucie and two of her cousins, Heddy

Uncle Sandor

13

Lucie, photographed by Uncle Sandor, between cousins Heddy and Kathe, on their visit to Capri in 1922.

and Kathe, with him on trips across Europe. He was a good, stylish skier, and also took Lucie and her cousins with him to Switzerland, in particular to St Moritz. Lucie later regretted that she never went with him to South America and the Amazon, but they went on cultural expeditions to the Loire, Toulouse, Aix-en-Provence, Paris and Sicily. Their travelling was done at the same time as that of the Viennese Oscar Kokoschka, and often they visited the very same places, such as Aigues Mortes on the Rhone Delta, although on their travels they never met.

Lucie, left, with Uncle Sandor and a worker in the vineyard.

Sandor was to stir Lucie's interest in classical archaeology and architecture. It was in his collection, taken from local excavations in his own vineyards, that she first saw and appreciated Roman pottery, particularly some fine-rimmed bowls, with springing profiles. His enthusiasm for the excellent in art and in craft was infectious. In influencing the niece who in later age so closely resembles him in facial expression, Sandor thus had his own small influence on contemporary pottery. He was a talented amateur, who was immortalized as 'Herr von Weil' in one of the novels of Franz Werfel, the last husband of Alma Mahler.

In a biography of Lucie Rie it is hard to resist the temptation to digress briefly, and give a few more details of the life and influence of her favourite uncle. In Eisenstadt he shared, as a young man, responsibility with his elder brother Leopold for the production of the wine. It was carefully divided into kosher wine, made only by Jewish Orthodox workers (gentiles were not even allowed to go near the store) and non-kosher wine, of which there was much more. As a businessman Sandor was able to arrange for export to Romania, and even the Papal States. A sympathetic aristocrat, a pillar in the town, he managed to get on with most people, Jew and Gentile, but not with the Esterhazys. There were quarrels with the Esterhazy's bailiff over the use of land. Right by the Wolf's house was the Esterhazy Mayerhof Dairy. This building, with its row of dairymen's cottages, is to this day like a backdrop to a Hungarian operetta, but through its great arched entrance Lucie and the other grandchildren never went: it would have been an indiscretion to visit.

Sandor was not only responsible for the management of the estates in Eisenstadt: he also had property interests in Vienna, where he owned an apartment block. In the capital in winter he lived at No. 6 Falkstrasse, and he described himself as director of the Burgenlandisches Museum. This may have been for the benefit of enlarging his collection of local cultural artefacts: Eisenstadt was the capital of the district of Burgenland. He extended his interests to traditional architecture, and acted as a civil servant with the government department concerned with the repair of old buildings.

When Jewish families came under threat in the 1930s, he managed to retain a certain amount of influence and power. Finally, beaten up and put in prison in Vienna by the Nazis, he organized his own 'leave' from time to time, to attend to business matters in Budapest and elsewhere, whilst at the same period striking up friendships with the other prisoners. Some of these were common thieves, and they promised Sandor that, when they were released, they would use their burglary skills to reclaim for him certain items from his collection which had been taken over by the Nazis. Sandor and one of his sisters and some nieces reached Israel before the Holocaust – in fact the Nazis gave Sandor Wolf his railway ticket to Tel Aviv – and he lived in Haifa until his death in 1946.

Naturally enough, after the Second World War, there were no Wolfs left in Eisenstadt. All the Jewish families were dispersed. But the Nazis had used the Wolfs' house as their headquarters, and this massive family home and the collection it contained remained almost undamaged, like the polygonal, walled Jewish cemetery nearby, which for some reason was also left intact throughout the Nazi occupation. When the time came to reassess the situation after the war, the Austrian state had to decide whether or not to keep the Wolf collection, which included Haydn manuscripts, for Austria. In the event the collection was sold to Switzerland, but the house was retained by the Burgenland, and now houses the official county museum, which covers everything from natural history and palaeontology to winemaking and beekeeping. Of its type it is a model, and alongside it is another building (which also once belonged to the Wolf family) housing the Austrian State Jewish Museum and Study Centre. Amongst other things, it celebrates with photography, letters and artefacts the life of Sandor Wolf as an historian of Zionism. Although the man was naturally interested in Zionism, his collection had been widespread in its coverage, and included many Christian artefacts, sarcophagi and pagan memorials, some of which were too heavy to move when the collection went to Switzerland, so they remained in the house.

Years later, in the 1960s, part of Alexander Wolf's collection of Jewish treasures – fine incense holders, torah covers and manuscripts – were bought back from Switzerland, and are now housed again in Eisenstadt, where unfortunately few people are old enough to remember the remarkable man who collected them.

The Wolf family house, used by the Nazis as their headquarters, and now the Burgenlandisches Museum.

The entrance to the Wiener Werkstätte exhibition in Berlin, 1904, designed by Josef Hoffmann and Koloman Moser.

Hoffmann

2 Vienna, the Secession, and the Wiener Werkstätte

An explosion in the visual arts and the polarization of new thought around a group of Viennese designers at the beginning of the twentieth century was inevitably part of the environment of Lucie Gomperz' childhood. The impact of this revolutionary thinking on the academically orientated Gomperz household was not particularly significant, but the art school which Lucie was to enter at the age of twenty was conditioned by the Vienna Secession of a quarter of a century earlier, and inextricably linked with the Wiener Werkstätte, founded a few months after Lucie was born.

Vienna was late in starting its artistic revolution. The Arts and Crafts Movement in England, and the Art Nouveau/*Jugendstil* of Western Europe predated it, but when it came it was more radical and more closely co-ordinated. Like most things Viennese, it was to thrive on dissension and rivalry, petty jealousies and personal vendettas. No rivalry was more bitter than that between Adolf Loos, architect and theorist, friend and mentor of Oscar Kokoschka, and Josef Hoffmann, architect, designer and co-founder of the Wiener Werkstätte. Both born in 1870, Loos was publishing his diatribe against vulgar ornamentation, *Potemkin's Town*, in the year of the Secession, 1898, the same year that Hoffmann was appointed to teach at the Kunstgewerbeschule – the school of arts and crafts – which Lucie later attended.

All over Vienna talented designers in coffee-house conclave were to plan together a new background for living, and a new direction for the fine arts. A total design philosophy was beaten out in an atmosphere where wealthy patrons would pay for a house to be designed down to the last knife and fork, and where rivals and collaborators would take pride in their competence to produce menu cards, posters, fabrics, wallpapers, light fittings, chairs, bureaux, glass, silver and ceramics.

With most of the major painters, including Kokoschka, teaching at the Kunstgewerbeschule, this school was at the hub of the visual and plastic arts – an enviable position for a school – in the years before the First World War. Hoffmann's dual role, as teacher at the school and founder with the designer Koloman Moser of the Wiener Werkstätte, gave him influence both in art theory and also in the world of marketing. The

Beechwood chair designed by Hoffmann, embodying the creative spirit of the early Wiener Werkstätte at its best.

Werkstätte was not only an organization of designers with similar ideals, it was a physical entity – a spacious building in the Neustiftgasse, with workshops for all the major crafts, a retail showroom, and Hoffmann's architectural practice alongside. From here he designed the building for the Kunstschau in 1908, and the Palais Stoclet in Brussels from 1905 to 1911.

Jane Kallir's detailed book *Viennese Design and the Wiener Werkstätte* documents the rise and fall of the Werkstätte from its foundation in 1903 to its final demise in 1932. She writes, 'Through their connections with Vienna's Kunstgewerbeschule the leaders of the Wiener Werkstätte established a chain of influence that ran through the lives of all the major artistic innovators of pre-war (1914–18) Vienna. . . . There is hardly an aspect of life or art that the Wiener Werkstätte did not touch, hardly an artist who, growing up in Vienna in the years before World War I, was not affected in some way by it.'

It is interesting that Lucie's parents when Lucie was a girl went there to do their 'special' shopping, much as they might have gone to Heal's or Liberty's in England, and that when Lucie's father decided to rebuild his surgery after the family moved to the Falkstrasse, he employed the Werkstätte designer Eduard Wimmer to furnish it for him in the fashionable style.

The abundance of design talent in the early years of Lucie's life was quite dazzling. Like exotic and colourful butterflies of infinite variety, the products of the Wiener Werkstätte designers to adorn the house and the body appeared everywhere in galleries, studios, buildings and homes. Furniture, glass and jewellery, especially by Koloman Moser and Dagobert Peche, and dress fabrics, designs and accessories of stunning originality, made Vienna at this time the creative centre of Europe.

One major area of applied design failed to achieve the same level of vitality, and this was ceramics. Although the distinguished designer Berthold Löffler had founded in 1906 the Wiener Keramik with Michael Powolny (the man who was later to become Lucie's tutor), both Löffler and his other collaborators were designers, not executors, and there was a need for a potter with vision to complement the brilliant designers in other fields. When Koloman Moser, who preferred to work in metal, glass and wood, turned his considerable talents to ceramics, it was with a broad decorative flourish which ignored the potential of the medium, and both he and Berthold Löffler, who was really a graphic designer, expected pottery glazes to be the obedient servants of the designer rather than almost animate and inspirational.

Powolny, the co-founder of Wiener Keramik, was a peasant potter through and through, and was not the right man to help raise the status of pottery in a Vienna suddenly devoted to radical reappraisal of decoration and design. His training in traditional and decorative ware was too ingrained, and he either would not or could not open his mind to more fundamental sculptural approaches. Coming from a family associated with the making of ceramic stoves, he was an expert technician, and took on a position of great potential influence when he became the director of ceramics at the Kunstgewerbeschule in 1909. But, as has already been said, his vision was limited and when the first impetus of the foundation of the Wiener Keramik had gone, designers such as Löffler seemed to lose interest, and the pottery reverted to whimsical, decorative, non-functional porcelain of the 'little boy rides on a snail' variety, which really had more to do with the Empire style attacked by Loos than the Secession and what came after.

In the absence of other significant potters, the well-intentioned Powolny had a negative influence on ceramics. He was out of his depth. Strong on technical matters and ceramic chemistry he was valued by his students, and liked as a gentle and kindly figure. But his more dynamic colleagues, especially Hoffmann, poked fun at him and enjoyed exploiting his weakness for alcohol by encouraging him to get drunk. (On the occasion of his one visit to England, he had to be escorted home by a London policeman because of drunkenness.)

It is hard to believe that, clever technician though he may have been, Powolny had any clear idea of what ceramics were about in the twentieth century. Even when working with the more dynamic and austere Löffler, his partner, their work never rose above the *kleinkunst*, and to many the personal output of this bewildered man is dire. But his gentleness preserved him and protected him from the vitriolic backbiting — the poisonous snapping and scrapping of the Viennese creative world of the time. He probably had few, if any, real enemies. John Houston, kindly disposed to the Powolny-inspired work of the Wiener Keramik, has written, 'They are charming . . . in the same way that the decorative moulded or modelled biscuits and bread of folk craft owe some of their interest to the sharper forms of wood and metal that they imitate. . . . Aesthetically and socially these ceramics depend on

Michael Powolny

19

A post-war picture of the Kunstgewerbeschule: today the buildings remain the same, but the address is now Oskar Kokoschka-Platz.

the viewer's complicity in a little knowing coquetry.' One cannot imagine either the man or his work standing up against the austere design strictures of a man like Adolf Loos. Yet Lucie, when she entered the school in 1922, really liked and respected him.

Perhaps the Gomperz family slightly indulged their youngest child. As a pupil she showed a tendency towards science subjects, and both her parents and Lucie herself at one time thought she would have a technical education and later a career in medicine. But her special tutor for drawing, Oscar Reiner, encouraged her to enter the Kunstgewerbeschule. She actually felt she was letting her parents down by preferring this 'less serious' training when the decision was made. However, the Kunstgewerbeschule was just down the road from the Falkstrasse, so Professor Gomperz's daughter at least would not have to cross Vienna on her way to and fro.

The original buildings are still used, and the appearance of these lofty rooms cannot be very different today from that of 1922. Lucie enrolled in September of that year, and although she had been encouraged by Reiner to study sculpture, she was expecting to do a general art course. When she saw the potter's wheel on the first day, in her own words she 'was lost to it'. Apart from a certain amount of life drawing and art history, she specialized in ceramics and has maintained her enthusiasm for, and fidelity to, wheel-thrown pottery ever since.

It was a small department – only six or seven students,

Life-size pottery figure, made by Lucie to the design of Grete Salzer.

20

all girls – and Michael Powolny alone was in charge. Apparently, without her knowledge, he took Lucie's first finished pot and had it exhibited in the Palais Stoclet in Brussels – quite an accolade for a beginner. Lucie regretted that she missed the 'terrible Kokoschka' (who had even lectured briefly at Lucie's Gymnasium the year before she arrived) but her work attracted the attention of Hoffmann and his assistant Oswald Haertl, and Powolny made a point of taking her to exhibitions and museums.

Her termly reports are filled out in Powolny's handwriting. She was a diligent student, excelling both in application and output, but the reports are lifeless and dull. One of her contemporary students, Lisi Krippl, remembers Lucie as hardworking, and she co-operated with another student, Grete Salzer, in making the life-size standing ceramic figure shown opposite. Salzer was a sculptor, and responsible for the design, while Lucie carried it out by throwing and joining several large pieces. It is the only non-functional, decorative piece of ceramic she made.

Her work on the wheel had a straightforwardness which implied a functional philosophy, but really had little to do with functionalism. She had absorbed the early Secession/Werkstätte concept of design mothered and fathered by architecture, where everything that forms part of life, from wallpaper design to chairs and greeting cards, should relate back to architecture as its frame, and must be harmonious. Her pots were deceptively simple: cylinders and bowls. She was learning techniques and the behaviour of her raw materials, and with characteristic determination was scraping together a knowledge of chemistry that would help her to achieve the bright glaze colours which Powolny said were impossible. 'Look at that,' Powolny would say, 'Isn't it beautiful? But no-one can do it today.' Lucie took up the challenge, experimented with chemicals, overloading glazes with oxides, but noting and controlling the resulting pockmarked surfaces and making the first 'volcanic' glaze which later became one of her trademarks.

She must have gone back again and again to the red-clay Roman pots of Uncle Sandor's collection. She wanted to make pots for the *house* (significantly she

The Kunstgewerbeschule's copy of Lucie Gomperz' leaving certificate, June 1926.

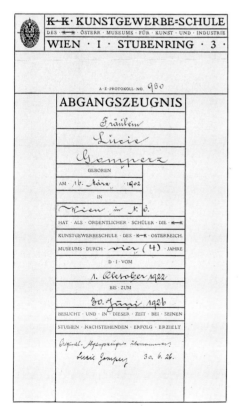
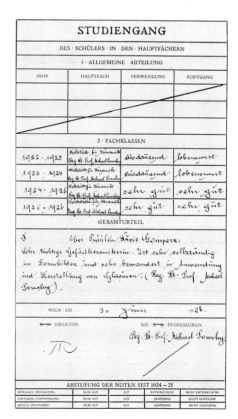

uses the word house rather than for *use*) and although she occasionally used clay 'rope' handles on pots to carry flower posies, and cusped shapes which could have been moulded, there were few concessions in her work to the figurative dimpled cherubs of Powolny. Having caught the eye of Hoffmann and Haertl, who put her pots into the Werkbund exhibition, she was, in 1925, being exhibited in Paris.

During Lucie's student years, the reputation and influence of the Werkstätte were crumbling. That Lucie should remember the Werkstätte most clearly as a place where she and her mother went to get their Christmas presents indicates just how, by the 1920s, these distinguished workshops linked with her own art school had lost status, and also the ephemeral direction in which they were going. Having started by attracting together multi-talented artists and designers the Werkstätte suffered as one by one they left. It was rather better at attracting talents than in training them, and although in the 1920s the original founding figure of Hoffmann was still in charge, most of the designers in many fields were women. In chauvinistic style critics laid the blame at their door for the descent of the Werkstätte output from pioneering masterworks to artsy-craftsy *kleinkunst*. In the area of ceramics the best known – Suzi Singer, Vally Wieselthier, Hilda Jesser, and Powolny himself – were producing decorated *kitsch*, articles of winsome charm from which Lucie turned away with instinctive disgust.

England has never had a teacher/designer quite like Hoffmann. For thirty years or more this energetic, multi-talented man held sway, whilst forging a convenient link between the Kunstgewerbeschule and

Left: Lucie in her studio in Wollzeile. The accompanying photographs show her work from the early 1930s, fired to earthenware temperatures, and either simple or subtle, according to one's point of view.

the Werkstätte, which gave his students a direct and easy passage from learning their craft to marketing their designs. One effect, of course, was that the output of the Werkstätte varied in quality according to the quality of the students, and by the time Lucie was herself going there to buy occasional Christmas presents,

its products had the half-baked air of immediate post-student work.

After graduating, Lucie herself exhibited some work in the Werkstätte, but found it displayed 'reluctantly' and never sold a single piece. With hindsight, the reason is pretty obvious. Lucie's work made no concessions to the whimsical folk art fashion; it was altogether too spartan and severe. In spirit it belonged to the earlier years when the Wiener Werkstätte had a philosophy.

Hoffmann clearly appreciated this, and having sent her work to Paris in 1925, he ensured it went also to London, Milan, and Paris again during the years after she completed her studies. To the 1937 Paris International Exhibition, Hoffmann actually took and exhibited seventy pieces by Lucie, and the French grudgingly gave her a prize. Not the first prize, though: '*tous la même chose*' was their verdict.

During the years from 1926, Lucie in her work learned not to be diverted from a simple intention to make harmonious pots for the house, in which the form was kept extremely simple – bowl or cylinder – and the decoration consisted of glaze concoctions of a voluptuous and a chemically challenging kind. The photographs above and on pages 81–85 show some of the work and indicate that to be 'modern' in the 1930s did not necessarily mean to be strictly functional.

23

Above: Lucie skiing in St Anton; below: with cousins at Potzleinsdorf, 1919. Top right: sailing on Lake Molveno, Lucie in the centre.

Above: on the beach at Greifenstein, Lucie in the foreground, Hans Rie with the ball.

Lucie follows two other skiers on Piz Buin, on the Swiss–Austrian border.

3 Vienna: Marriage 1926-38

Lucie's elder brother Teddy was rather irritatingly protective. Five years older, he tended to monitor her friendships, and even listened in to conversations, but Lucie's student years saw increased independence, and most of her free time was spent in sport: canoeing, rock climbing, swimming, tennis and other sports, some of which are shown in the photographs here. They also show the grace and beauty of the girl, vivacious, but also serious. Her favourite sport was skiing. When Lucie and her friends went to the mountains to ski in the early years of this century, ski-lifts were almost non-existent. Ensuring an exhilarating run down meant a laborious climb up first, and there was a real pioneering spirit in the small groups that went, knapsacks on backs, into the Tyrol, the Dolomites, and in Lucie's case more often than not to Switzerland. Her favourite resort was St Anton, on the southern Italian border, and parties would spend several days on *randonnées*, staying overnight in mountain refuges – a combination of the mountain idyll with the daring and dangerous. Lucie's parents must either have relaxed their attitudes, or perhaps may not even have realized how risky such outings could be. The ski instructors then, as now, made the sport a glamorous and inviting one.

Rudi Matt, skier, skiing instructor and friend.

25

Ernst Rie

It was when she was quite a young girl – still a teenager – that Lucie first became aware of a dashing young doctor of physics, Ernst Rie, a good skier and a respected mountaineer. Lucie admired him from afar, and they were never really close friends. When they first met Lucie was still a schoolgirl, but he was courteous and kind to her. They were interested in the same sporting activities and Lucie remembers hearing about his leaving on a climbing trip to the Dachstein glacier with a friend, later both men to be reported missing. After some days Rie's young brother Hans went with the search party and came across the two climbers dead, frozen on a stone bench. A photograph of this good-looking climber is shown on the left. Lucie was struck with sadness for the loss of another man she admired.

Hans Rie did not have his brother's enquiring mind, but was an equally keen sportsman and a good skier. He and Lucie, closer in age, spent more and more time together, linked in sport. They became identified as a 'couple'. By 1925, a cousin was hinting to Lucie that she would have to marry Hans. The full implications of marriage do not seem to have struck Lucie at the time. It was just the logical progression of weekends and holidays spent together, and, after all, Hans Rie was an appropriately eligible bachelor. He had a technical-cum-managerial job in the felt-hat factory of the Brüder Böhm in Vienna and good prospects. Altogether it was a highly reasonable union in Jewish terms: two appropriate families getting together. But this is not quite what Lucie's cousin meant – she was really concerned that if Lucie and Hans did not marry, then the families might be facing scandalous talk . . . and so they were engaged.

Lucie with Hans Rie

Lucie in Lans, summer 1919.

Hans had, it seems, not taken all that much interest in Lucie's ceramics course at the Kunstgewerbeschule. Perhaps he did not think it was really a serious occupation. However, in the year 1926, with her diploma achieved in June, the couple were married in September and set off for a honeymoon in Taormina from Vienna station, with a certain amount of shaking of heads by those friends at the reception who had accompanied them thus far.

Honeymoon in Taormina

27

Of the many sorts of unsuccessful marriages, that of Lucie and Hans Rie was of the gentlest kind. There would have been no violent rows, or even acrimony, just a turning away from each other from the very start, with Hans increasingly absorbed in sporting pursuits and card-playing, convivial evenings with male friends, and Lucie, the home-maker, steadily developing an independence which has stood her in such good stead since. There was no alternative: either she would have left Hans for someone else, or she had to put up with her lot – a forlorn marriage of boredom – while she invoked the only foundation she had for an alternative life: her training as a potter.

Her contacts in the Viennese applied arts world, and the spirit of the time, helped her in this, although the greatest help came from a young architect, Ernst Plischke. At the beginning of a distinguished career he, like Lucie, had just qualified in the year 1926, and met Lucie simply because he was looking for pots which suited the design of a house he was building on the Attersee.

The youthful, compelling architect Ernst Plischke, designer of the Apartment Rie, shown below left.

He found Lucie an experienced, willing and intelligent potter; a receptive mind and a ready friend. Lucie in turn found the boyish Ernst intellectually stimulating and attractive – a complete contrast with the totally physical Hans Rie, and from their first meeting, when Ernst Plischke simply wanted to order some pots, a friendship grew. Lucie and Hans Rie had started their married life in Lucie's parents' house, but a few months into their marriage Uncle Sandor had placed an apartment in one of his properties, No. 24 Wollzeile, at their disposal. The Ries were on the point of moving in when Ernst Plischke appeared on the scene. Lucie, admiring a chair which was designed by the young Plischke, told him about the new apartment and soon he was commissioned to design the interior. This does not sound much of a commission for an aspiring architect, but it gave him the chance to put into practice his advanced theories about living space, predating those of the Bauhaus, which were not crystallized, after all, until 1929. The watercolours which exist of the apartment show just how seriously Plischke took the assignment, and the photographs of the finished flat prove his thoroughness. He measured Hans Rie's legs to get the proportions of the sofas

right, and the right height for the cupboards. Hans Rie's compliance and Lucie's pleasure in the project make this period, 1926 to 1928, an exciting time, and Lucie had a kiln installed in the apartment. She had previously been potting at home but, without a kiln, had to have her pottery fired elsewhere, taking it by tram across the city, wrapped in newspaper in a suit-case. Now she would be able to make pots for herself at home, while Plischke commissioned cabinet-makers and chair-makers to very precise briefs.

The young architect had many other concerns. His urbane, simple, stark buildings were very advanced for their time, and he was taken on to work in the office of Peter Behrens. Lucie's developing friendship with him received a jolt when he got married to his Jewish girlfriend Anna, and soon after, in early 1929, he left for America with high hopes of a share in the practice of William Muschenheim. It must have been quite a traumatic time for Lucie, who was left with the task of completing the Apartment Rie herself, and paying off the furniture makers. For Plischke, 1929 was hardly the year in which to arrive in America, and soon after the Wall Street Crash of October his hopes for an architectural career in America were dashed.

Faced with any disappointment, Lucie turned to her work and found fulfilment there, helped it must be said by some success both locally and internationally. The Wiener Werkstätte was staggering through its final period of instability, but there were other outlets

Lucie and Hans Rie motoring, Niederalpel, 1930.

Left: Lucie in the apartment and, above, in the studio.

for artists, some with Jewish connections. The well-known house of Lobmeyr took and exhibited Lucie's work, and the glass company Bimini, directed by the designer Fritz Lampl, and named after an island in a poem by Heine, also took on Lucie Rie's pottery, as did the non-Jewish 'Aryan' Werkbund. Lucie had some success in both these establishments, and also won gold medals at exhibitions in Brussels and Milan, as some ornate certificates testify (see page 34).

Photographs taken in the 1930s show a woman either serenely at her wheel at 24 Wollzeile, or enjoying holidays by the lakeside or in the mountains with her husband. But the period from 1926 to the *Anschluss* was a long one, and for Lucie it was not a happy time.

Lucie with her father at 24 Wollzeile, 1932.

As the years darkened with the coming of another war, anti-semitism in the city increased. Families who had been friends for years and years turned away from one another. Lucie's student friend Lisi Krippl told her, to her mystification, that there was a reason why she was not invited to a party. Lucie's days and nights were mainly spent working in her pottery. The photograph above shows her in her studio with her father, one of the last photographs taken of them together. Though he practised at the top of his profession even in his later years, Professor Gomperz fell victim to one of the Viennese misunderstandings between professional men. Somewhat younger than the great Sigmund Freud, nevertheless when Freud required the assistance of an ear, nose and throat specialist he always called in Professor Gomperz, until one day Gomperz 'forgot' to go to a Freud consultation over a patient and was never forgiven, or asked again. Lucie remembers meeting Freud when she was a teenager, and how kind he was to her then – 'intelligent, tactful, nice, unemotional' – but she only met him once more after she was married.

The 1930s were also for Lucie years of loss. Her grandmother Hermine Wolf died in 1932 at the age of 86. Not long afterwards, her father Benjamin Gomperz died of stomach cancer. Her mother Gisela suffered meningitis, and a period of uneasy mental instability, before she too died in November 1937, following a stroke. Lucie's elder brother Teddy, who had qualified as an engineer and worked for Ingersoll, departed suddenly, first to Budapest, then to the United States.

But Lucie's reputation was growing, in spite of the uneasy political situation, and numerous pots with her 'L.R.G. Wien' mark underneath must still be spread widely in Vienna and Europe; at least, those which have survived. Some of the best pots of this time – those which Lucie brought with her to England – are illustrated on pages 82–3.

One of Uncle Sandor's tenants at 24 Wollzeile was the distinguished Viennese photographer, Lotte Meitner-Graf, with her studio on the top floor. She and Lucie were not formally introduced, but one day they found themselves together in the lift. Soon Lucie received a message from a third party that Lotte Meitner-Graf was taken with her appearance, and wanted to photograph her. The Meitner-Graf reputation was so great – she was the best known portrait photographer in Vienna at the time – that prominent people in all walks of life came to the Wollzeile studio. Lucie did not like her, but luckily for posterity agreed to the sittings, and a series of marvellous portraits was the result. Dramatic and mannered poses with velvety lighting were typical of the period, not just of the Meitner-Graf style, but this gifted woman photographer was able to express exactly the air of disillusionment and sadness in the face and posture of her beautiful subject.

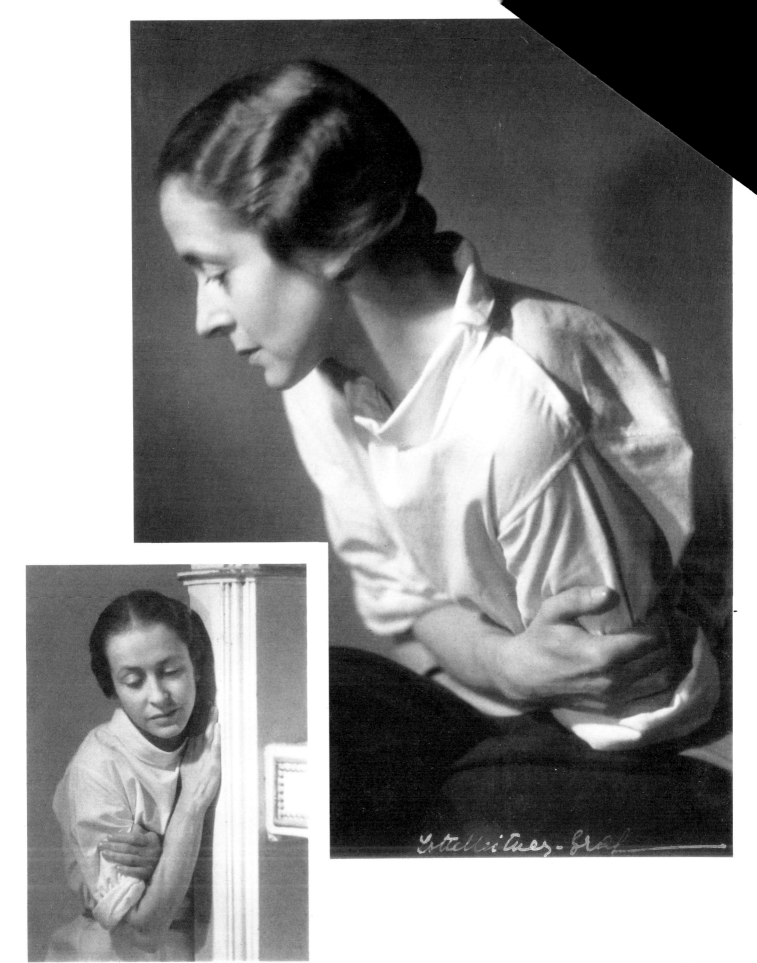

4 England in Wartime

Lucie as she leaves Vienna for England, 1938.

When Lucie came to England in October 1938 she left behind her a life of some comfort and style. Never interested in politics, she was emotionally less bruised by the vicious policies of Nazism than many Viennese, and probably less aware than most Jews of the terrifying time ahead for the Jewish community of which she was a part. She simply could not understand the sudden serious polarization of Viennese society, always in her words 'silly', against the entire Jewish community. Certain friends hung Nazi flags outside their windows and even the man who helped her with kiln firings wore a Nazi armband. To Lucie this extraordinary change of behaviour was incomprehensible, but it became obvious, in the late 1930s, that she and her husband had to leave.

There were only two options open to the Ries – England, or America *via* England – so it was to England that she came, like thousands of others as a refugee.

Her only surviving brother had already gone to America. She had lost both her parents. Her marriage was arid and empty. In England she knew hardly a soul, and did not even speak the language very well. Such a reversal of early fortunes could have been expected to depress her spirits, at the very least. It may seem perverse, but instead she knew that her life was just beginning. Everything that went before seemed to count for nothing. She was excited and happy, and she warmed to England. Though her opportunities were so limited, her horizons widened.

With hindsight it is easy to see that as a potter the break with Vienna, and the arrival in England, was the most important event in her creative life. She herself and her Viennese contemporaries agree that if she had stayed – if she had been able to stay and work – her achievement as a potter would have been much less: she would have been stifled. Her career would have been more that of an artisan than an artist. Coming

Theo Frankel, who became a lifelong friend.

to England was creatively a very liberating experience.

James Plaut, writing of Oscar Kokoschka who came to England in the same circumstances in 1938, said of him, 'He did not feel the constriction and provincialism of Vienna.' So with Lucie. Windows opened on a much wider world, though the process of establishing herself was long and painful. The resolution of this young and beautiful woman single-mindedly to work at what she wanted to do, seems to have strengthened in 1938 as the European nations prepared for war.

On one of the skiing expeditions in St Anton, Lucie and Hans Rie had met Theo Frankel, an energetic and talented technocrat who was already established in England by 1938, and it was he who vouched for the Ries as their sponsor and arranged their passage to London. Two thousand pounds was quite a substantial sum of money in 1938, and this is what Lucie and Hans brought with them when they arrived – of course, without a job – and lodged first in a boarding house in Hampstead before moving to a flat at No. 24 Frognal nearby, where they lived for nearly a year. A network of Viennese Jewish emigrés, intent on assisting their fellow countrymen, provided them with a circle of friends, most of them based in Hampstead, which was then just as it is now, a most fortunate part of London. Among these friends were Ernst Freud, the architect son of Sigmund, together with his wife, the Viennese artist Fritz Lampl, whose glass-blowing and retailing enterprise Bimini he had transferred to London, as well as the Ries' sponsor Theo Frankel, and one of Lucie's Viennese cousins, Franz Böhm.

Hans Rie quickly took up the challenge of helping refugees, and through the Ries' London home flowed a stream of Viennese Jews. Lucie was called upon to cook for them, but she was less actively involved than Hans, and in any case, her mind was on other things. While Hans was preparing for the second stage in their evacu-

ation – the move to America – Lucie was finding out as much as possible about the world of hand-made pottery in England, and looking for a studio of her own. There was no equivalent of the Wiener Werkstätte here, but there were the major art schools, there was Gordon Russell and his circle, and there was the Victoria and Albert Museum with the ceramics department directed by William Honey. And there was the refined Little Gallery in Chelsea, run by Muriel Rose and laid out like a well-bred country house, with overtones of the Arts and Crafts Movement. It was at the Little Gallery that early in 1939 Lucie was introduced to Bernard Leach, who wanted to talk to her about many things, and took her for coffee to a cafeteria nearby. Lucie's meeting and subsequent friendship with Bernard Leach were of immense importance to both her personally and to her career, but she remembers feeling self-conscious on this day because she was wearing a tiny hat like a Viennese cake.

Although she had certificates and prizes from at least four international exhibitions in Europe in the 1930s, and had exhibited in London in 1934, her cosmopolitan reputation as a potter from the continent of Europe was barely established, cut no ice at all in England, and was to die away completely before she rebuilt it in her adopted country. It is hard to imagine, but when she met Bernard Leach her previous achievements as a potter counted for nothing at all. He had never heard of her or her work, but he was obviously attracted to the elegant young Viennese woman herself, who responded warmly to his particular brand of erudition. She showed him some of her Viennese pots, which on such occasions she carried round in a suitcase. He had nothing really positive to say about her ceramics – which must have baffled him. They were 'too thickly glazed', 'too thinly potted', 'too much like stoneware', 'not stoneware enough', they 'had no humanity', they

33

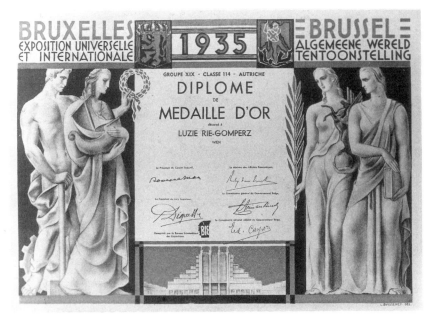

One of a number of historic certificates gained by Lucie Rie Gomperz.

'were not humble', and so on, and so on. Pretty devastating for Lucie, who was far from unaware of the reputation of Leach. Yet he clearly wanted to know more about the intriguing refugee and soon asked her to visit him at his pottery.

How different was the reaction she got when she visited William Staite-Murray at the Royal College of Art, the other great figure in pre-war ceramics in England.

By contrast with the patrician Leach, who invested the craftsman with 'noble savage' status, Staite-Murray was an impatient, arrogant self-publicist, and it is not surprising that the two men did not see eye to eye. Lucie wanted a referee, someone to vouch for her as a potter, as a respectable craftswoman, in order to get a work permit, and she went to the man at the top – the equivalent of Powolny in Vienna, but quite a different character. She well remembers Staite-Murray's hands, firmly behind his back, when he said, 'We do not shake hands in England,' and for the second significant time she learned that whatever reputation she had had in Vienna, she had left it behind her. 'When are you going to start making pots?' was the only other memorable sentence at their one and only meeting. It is hard to know if he was being flippant, deliberately rude, or simply asking a practical question of a refugee. He gave her the signature that she wanted, but offered no help, and she realized she would have to live on her wits.

Mr William Honey of the Victoria & Albert Museum was rather more generous, and in particular his Quaker wife was able to exert some considerable influence later when the question of internment arose. Mean-while, Lucie, months into her new life in England, took positive action. She started to walk the streets of London in search of a workshop, preferably one with living accommodation, and she did not tell Hans Rie about it. She saw his imminent departure for America as a means of escape for herself, for she would not be going with him, and the thirteen-year-old marriage would shortly come to an end. With most of London strange, how she found herself in a mews on the northern borders of Hyde Park one can only guess, but here she found a garage workshop, with limited living accommodation over it, and she arranged to rent it from the Church Commissioners, who were informed that she wanted to use it as a pottery studio. With ecclesiastical pernicketyness, the Church Commissioners were at pains to insist that it be 'high-class pottery'. Perhaps they were afraid of a plethora of toby jugs tarnishing the freeholders' reputation, but Lucie took the condition in rather good part. Indeed she appreciated the Church Commissioners' concern and found their approbation of her plans reassuring. So began the half-century relationship with Albion Mews, which in the 1930s was a rundown backwater, which fell on even harder times during the war, but which has since increased relentlessly in stature and status decade by decade, oblivious of Lucie and her work.

In early 1939 the helpful Ernst Freud was made privy to her plans for the garage, and assisted her in re-shaping the upstairs apartment as a flat for one, organizing and accommodating the Plischke-designed functional furniture and cupboarding which Lucie managed to have shipped, at great expense, from the Wollzeile flat in Vienna.

A visitor at Lucie's newly converted workshop.

Much has been written about the severe but serene beauty of this really rather small flat in Albion Mews. It is quite difficult to assess how much is the effect of the Plischke furniture, and how much that of a sensitive architect – Freud – in supervising the living arrangements of his Austrian friend. In modern estate agents' terms it would be described as a one-room flat. But it is elegant and seems spacious, and certainly carries across to England the principle of living space propounded by Plischke, and pursued by him throughout his long career.

While the paint was still drying on the walls of her future home in Albion Mews, Lucie set off to Devon, where she had been invited to stay for a week at Dartington Hall with Bernard Leach. The Shinners Bridge Pottery at Dartington, nursery to a number of significant potters, is indeed an idyllic place by the clear River Dart. It, and the long conversations she had with Bernard Leach, made an immense impression on Lucie, who was daily aware of liberation from intimidation and political persecution, from the narrowness of thought of her Austrian pottery contemporaries and, rather more guiltily, she anticipated her forthcoming liberation from a failed marriage.

Leach was already established, and about halfway through his long career. He had just completed the manuscript of his influential book, *A Potter's Book*. He was worried about the political clouds menacing Europe: war was inevitable, he said. He was also worried, unnecessarily as it turned out, about the timing of his book's publication: 'Like hatching an egg in a thunderstorm.'

Leach's years in Japan and his dedication through

Albion Mews

his years of pottery had made him a master, and Lucie now saw clay handled with the flowing rhythm of a natural craftsman, a far cry from the self-conscious kunstschule tactics of Vienna. In addition, Leach provided the intellect which she appreciated in Plischke, but had never expected or hoped for from her teacher Powolny. Leach seemed to combine experience and craftsmanship with an enquiring mind free from professional jealousies and personality problems. With this man you did not have to make allowances; you could listen and soak it all up. Bernard Leach always needed an audience, and Lucie provided him with an eager listener as they spent long tea-breaks literally on the little bridge over the River Dart, discussing everything under the sun.

That Bernard Leach single-handed saved the art of handmade pottery in England from extinction is something of a myth. There were plenty of country potteries in action all over England in the 1920s and 30s, although the master potters were unrecognized and their status was not high. What Leach did in the years between the wars, through the force of his personality, was to bring handmade pottery to the attention of influential people and patrons, and to enlist their help in obtaining status for the potter by a rather curious route. He promoted the image of the potter as someone of *moral* superiority, not an artist, but a 'master' with aesthetic sensitivity and access, if you wish, to a transcendental experience. To be a potter needed dedication – it was certainly hard work. Patrons of the arts, such as the Elmhirsts of Dartington, were enlisted as supporters, and the economic climate of the 1930s was such that Leach's particular brand of craftsmanship gained hand-picked followers. He preached and his disciples followed. Leach's profile was high, but his circle was small.

All of this changed with the publication of *A Potter's Book*. A beautifully written and personal account of life as a potter, mainly set in Japan and Britain, it had and still has a universal appeal which extended the awareness of pottery to a general audience, whilst at the same time more closely identifying Leach's name with the cause of hand-made ceramics.

Lucie needed no encouragement to stick to her chosen craft, but Leach was a disturbing influence on her because his views on the basic elements of good pottery were uncompromising and in conflict with her own work. They did not allow for cross-breeds. William Honey had already said to Lucie that she made earthenware that looked like stoneware, and Lucie,

confused, cast around for new guidelines when she returned to London. By now her workshop in Albion Mews was equipped with her small top-loading kiln designed in Vienna by a maker of dentists' kilns, and her two wooden continental wheels. Here she was to start to make pottery again.

Meanwhile she had to break the news to Hans that she had found a flat, organized it so that she could live there with the Vienna furniture, but alone. It was not big enough (thank goodness) for two, and Hans was free to go to New York. Since Lucie had never ceased to like and respect Hans this was a difficult moment. He cannot have been very happy in the marriage, but he was hurt that she had somehow deceived him with her plans and was now urging him to go on to New York. He left, handing her the rest of the money. £1400 was left out of the original £2000, and he sailed for Boston in autumn 1939.

No sooner had Lucie moved into Albion Mews than the war broke out, and her first months there were spent living with blackout curtains, anticipating, together with everyone else, civilian bombing. Meeting up with Fritz Lampl, who was bravely attempting to set up the Bimini workshop again, gave Lucie both warm friendship and a job, for Lampl suggested that Lucie should help him in his Soho workshop in Great Chapel Street, pressing glass buttons for women's clothes by melting glass rods and using moulds based on a variety of subjects, including Roman coins from the British Museum. Lucie tried her hand at glass blowing, but without much enthusiasm or success, and divided her time between glass button-making in Soho and ceramics in her own studio.

In the early days of the war, it may seem odd that an archery club flourished in the field adjacent to St George's churchyard, which backed on to Lucie's studio in Albion Mews. The clubhouse of the archers was in the mews itself, and one member, interested, strayed across the road and into Lucie's pottery almost as soon as she had started work there. He was Stanley North, an artist and picture restorer at Hampton Court, who lived nearby in Ladbroke Grove. Lucie remembers feeling that from the moment he stepped into the studio he never really left. A friendship between the two quickly grew. He bought her first pots – a series of earthenware jugs – and later returned them to her saying that they belonged in Albion Mews (where they still are today, see page 219). He enlisted her help with his own projects, which involved ceramic tiles. He tried pottery himself, and he designed an 'LR' seal for her pots. He just wanted to work with Lucie. How Bernard Leach took the arrival of this man on to the scene one can only guess, but certainly Lampl, Lucie's other great supporter at the time, got on well with Stanley North and at the end of the working day Stanley would go from Albion Mews to accompany Fritz Lampl to Paddington Station through the darkened wartime streets. Since both of them suffered from night blindness, it would have been more useful if Lucie had gone instead.

Lampl was married and living in Hampstead. Stanley North was married, but his wife and son were in South Africa and he was living alone in Ladbroke Grove. He had an inventive turn of mind and for one of his projects to assist in the war effort he needed ceramic tiles with holes in them, and he and Lucie worked together in Albion Mews to produce the prototypes by hand.

Lucie wrote to Hans Rie in Boston and asked him to organize their divorce in Arizona, because this was a great deal easier than in wartime London. Hans Rie could then, too, feel a free man and he complied. Rather a touching exchange of photographs in 1940 illustrates better than words their change in situation and fortune. Lucie sits alone in her sparse room north

Lucie in her flat and, above right: Hans Rie by the side of his car at Haverhill, Massachusetts.

of Hyde Park. Hans Rie, starting a new life in Massachusetts, stands alongside an amazing car, with his American friends inside and its folding hood in the air. When the photograph was taken he had recently been appointed manager of a felt-manufacturing company in Massachusetts, as a result of the reputation he had brought with him from Europe. He also sent Lucie a press cutting of the appointment, which she kept, delighted that her ex-husband had at least a good job. With official ties cut, the couple were able to maintain a friendly and steady contact, as Hans prospered and later remarried. It is interesting that this phlegmatic and sport-loving emigré from Vienna was actually 'head-hunted' for his technical expertise as soon as he arrived in America, and he was swiftly to rise to run the company and later to make history by selling its equity to its own workers. He even employed his brother-in-law Victor Böhm, who had once been his superior at Brüder Böhm Hats in Vienna.

In the early days of the bombing, Lucie had sought shelter by sleeping in the crypt of the nearby St George's Chapel, and found the warmth of feeling expressed towards her by the others in this air-raid shelter, in spite of her strong German accent, most reassuring. As refugees in Britain were suddenly all described as enemy aliens under Churchill's internment policy, Lucie had reason to thank the Quakers, and in particular the Quaker wife of William Honey of the Victoria & Albert Museum, who interceded on her behalf, so that she was spared this time of humiliation. Grateful and ready to show her loyalty to her adoptive country, Lucie tried to join several different Home Defence forces. She became an air-raid warden, and was issued with a helmet but given nothing much in the way of training. She tried to join a course held locally to train officers in how to deal with the population in the event of a poison gas attack, but she was turned away because she was foreign. In view of the language difficulties and her German accent, one can understand the recruiting officer's point of view, but Lucie was distressed. She became a fire watcher instead, and was issued with an axe and a bucket. She also had a stirrup-pump, but was not sure how to use it.

She remembers with amusement how bewildered she felt at the prospect of having to tackle a fire single-handed, thus armed, but that was the fire watcher's job. As the bombs started to fall in earnest, Lucie spent three nights a week on watch. Perhaps it was at this time that Lucie developed her acute sense of the absurd.

Sometimes she would stay late working in the button factory in Soho and it was fortunate that on one night in 1941 she went home to Albion Mews, for a foray by German bombers produced a direct hit on the Great Chapel Street premises, and when she visited the site the next day with Fritz Lampl only Lucie's apron, on its peg on a solitary wall, was left of the Bimini factory. It must have been a terrible blow to Fritz Lampl's hopes for re-establishing his work in Britain. The facilities for glass making are difficult to get together at the best of times, and at the beginning of the London Blitz, almost impossible. A new temporary workshop was set up in Epping Forest, but this involved a great deal of travelling, and Lucie was unwell. She caught diptheria and spent some time in hospital. When the bombing of London was at its height, Hans Rie wrote to Lucie from Boston suggesting that she should come to America for her own safety. 'You do not have to live with me,' he wrote, and was really concerned about his ex-wife, and she appreciated this. One bomb fell in Albion Mews, taking out all the windows. Lucie got a government-issue steel table, with concrete legs, and sheltered under it during the air-raids. Bernard Leach would join her there when the sirens caught him out on his fortnightly visits to London. A recurrence of a medical problem for which Lucie had had an operation in Vienna took her back into hospital, and this time she

stayed in for six weeks. While she was there, Stanley North, already ill with cancer, was also taken to hospital and the bright friendship which had so quickly grown between the two was to be extinguished. Three days after Lucie came out of hospital, Stanley North died of lung cancer. This man had become the most important person in Lucie's life, and she went to his dignified but poorly attended Buddhist funeral while really ill herself. In wartime his own family could hardly reach England from South Africa. Lucie was ill and weak, and the Dartington idyll of 1939 with Leach and the happy early days in Albion Mews in 1940 with Stanley North had turned swiftly, by 1941, into a time of deep sadness. Not since her brother Paul had died in 1917 had Lucie felt such a personal loss.

Lucie was much supported by Fritz Lampl, who had moved his glass workshop back to London, to nearby Sussex Gardens, and by the regular visits of Bernard Leach on Crafts Council business, a guest in Lucie's flat who, when not under her steel table, slept on her couch.

Lampl had a partner in his glass-buttons business — a Mr Schenker — and he encouraged Lucie to combine her newly-found button-making experience with her ceramic skills, and to make pottery buttons for haute couture. This change of emphasis, brought about by economic necessity, produced some remarkable work, extending to jewellery — earrings and necklaces. Some examples, brilliant with gold, are shown on pages 86–7.

For the one and only period in her life Lucie was producing work in the spirit of the Wiener Werkstätte. She drew on the technical knowledge she had learned at the Kunstgewerbeschule. Powolny, alive in Austria, but too old for active service, would have approved. Schenker could see the commercial potential of these exquisite buttons and jewellery, and set to work to organize Lucie as an efficient cottage industry. When she had come out of hospital in 1941 she had found yet another Austrian, the young Rudi Neufeldt, installed by Schenker in Albion Mews, making moulds and pressings for Lucie's approval. Another assistant was drafted in, and just as the operation began to get into its stride it was closed down by the government. The Board of Trade regarded it as non-essential industry, and the staff and Lucie herself were put to war work.

The optical industries factory of Hilger and Watts in Camden Town was where Lucie did her war effort. The adjusting of optical instruments replaced button-making, and Lucie was paid three pounds ten shillings per week. She worked hard during the day, but got up early and worked late at night at home making

Lucie in her workshop, with button moulds on the bench beside her, and below: some of the heavy earthenware made under the influence of Bernard Leach.

buttons in order to earn some more money. There is very little extant pottery from this period, which is probably just as well since she was still trying to digest Bernard Leach's ideas and his enthusiasm for robust peasant-ware, with the result that her work became thicker and unnecessarily clumsy. It was probably the worst pottery of her whole career. Leach's influence had knocked her off course. While she did not try to copy him, she could not help being influenced by his fluent throwing, his strong English/Oriental shapes, and his marvellous glazes. What could she do but follow? She was attracted by ash glazes, but unable to use them, as her kiln would not reach a high enough temperature for them to vitrify. She tried pouring glazes rather than painting them on, but this had a curious blanketing effect on her forms. She tried making thicker handles but these only looked crude. It is not that the Leach-influenced pots are bad, or even dull. They are interesting, but they are not pure Lucie. Indeed, when Bernard Leach spoke of Lucie to other friends at this time, he described her as 'the button-maker from Vienna'.

Once again Lucie's place of work was destroyed when the Hilger and Watts factory in Camden Town had a direct hit from a flying bomb – the pilotless plane known as a doodlebug. Luckily the manager was able to shepherd Lucie, together with the rest of the staff, into the cellar just before the bomb fell. Lucie took pride in her work in the spectographic department, and continued in a makeshift workshop scrambled together within the bombed ruins right up to the end of hostilities. She even took her turn as night watchman at the optical factory in the dying days of the war.

The nearest Lucie came during the 1940s to the languid days of relaxation on the Brunnerwiese were occasional outings to Dorking, where another Viennese friend, Bertl Saxl, had a cottage, and they went for walks in the woods looking for mushrooms – a subject on which Lucie was an expert. Of course Lucie's circle of friends increased during the war, which brought people of all sorts together, but after the death of Stanley North she did not have a close English companion. She sought the company and conversation of intelligent expatriates like herself, and waited for the day when the Government would let her reopen her ceramics 'factory' in Albion Mews. This was not to be until the end of 1945, after six months of trying.

5 England after the War

To George Wingfield Digby, Keeper of Textiles at the Victoria and Albert Museum, Lucie said in the 1950s, 'Bernard suddenly made me realize what you could see in a pot.' He came with his conviction that pottery was a serious business at a critical time for Lucie. The disorientation of being uprooted from her native country, and her rejection of her own marriage, left her really quite vulnerable and lacking in confidence, and standing in need of support.

Any description of Lucie at any time is always a conjunction of opposites, and if she was determined at the time she sought her own workshop, equally she clung gratefully for support to the person whose conviction of the importance of pottery reinforced her own. It must be remembered that this was a time of war, when the making of mere 'things' could seem slight and pointless, and even selfish, while lives were being sacrificed and families destroyed all around. So Bernard Leach's enthusiasm and help were quite vital, but the confusion he engendered because of his enthusiasm for a particular type of pot was also quite overwhelming. As a 'cause' for which it was worth her maintaining her independence, her conviction that pottery was worthwhile was reinforced, even if at the end of the war she was not sure what kind of pottery to make.

Muriel Rose had done her best to pair up Bernard Leach with Lucie before and during the war. As a match it would have been a disaster, at least for posterity, for Lucie's pottery would probably never have developed at all. She pots with a devotion and attention which excludes anything else important. A second marriage to a man like Bernard Leach would have absorbed that attention and left nothing free for pottery. Whether or not Lucie saw things in this light is irrelevant, since she never saw Bernard's friendship as a prelude to marriage, and as the war was ending he married Laurie Cookes instead. Bernard's second wife was rather put out by his attachment to Lucie and so for a time at least Lucie saw very little of Bernard Leach. She had absorbed his views on pottery and wondered at his skill, but as we have seen she was not able to bring her own pottery into line with his.

Lucie's friendship with Bernard Leach set her own work back several years. Hans Coper's arrival put her back on the right lines again. He allowed her and encouraged her to test her inventiveness and make what came naturally to her.

Hans Coper, a refugee from Saxony, who had lived through the war in considerable privation, appeared on Lucie's doorstep in 1946. He had no training in pottery but Lucie took him on as an assistant in her re-opened button factory and found him an efficient worker. He joined a cosmopolitan team composed almost entirely of refugees. English was the only language spoken in the workshop, although there were no English workers there. Hans quickly showed such application and such interest in clay that Lucie introduced him to her pottery-making techniques as well as button-making. When they met, Lucie was 44 and Hans was 26, an uneasy half-generation gap in their ages which both restrained and cemented the friendship which was to be of such significance to both until Hans's death in 1981. When Lucie makes friends they stay her friends, for she is immensely loyal, but up to the end of the Second World War she had had little luck with the men who mattered in her life – all of them had died or gone far away. Even Ernst Plischke had, in 1939, gone to New Zealand, and she had waved goodbye to her husband.

In meeting with Hans Coper, Lucie was to start the most important, and enduring, friendship of her life. Hans was very quiet about the place. Bernard Leach later wrote, 'She has this rather odd man who works there.' At first Hans rarely spoke at all, but he had the kind of intelligent eyes that make the bumptious feel

Colette du Plessis, Kitty Rix, Lucie and Ralph Meyer outside the workshop.

uneasy, and in his careful English, for he never spoke German if he could avoid it, he told Lucie enough about his life and situation for her to feel a great surge of sympathy for the man, half Jewish, who had suffered so much more than she had and with whom she knew she shared an identity of views. One warm summer day they talked for so long in Hyde Park that the park-keepers shut the gates on them, and they had to climb over the railings to get back home.

But Hans was married, and had the concerns of a young man with young children, and so the social time they spent together was brief, although they worked more and more on joint pottery projects. Hans' skill in handling clay astonished her, and soon he was staying on to make pots in the evenings after making buttons all day.

Hans Coper and Lucie at work in Albion Mews.

The workforce sometimes grew, and then shrank again, not so much according to the demand for buttons, but according to who was around: a French girl, a Japanese girl, and several Austrians, including Kitty Rix, who had learnt ceramics like Lucie at the Kunstgewerbeschule, and had in fact quite a reputation at the Werkstätte. A most significant arrival at the workshop was the German Jupp Dernbach, whose organizing skills and creativity made Albion Mews more productive. Plaster moulds were now used to produce ceramic buttons much faster: two hundred could be made in the time it took to make seventy by hand. One gets the impression that Hans and Jupp ganged up on Lucie sometimes when there was a question of policy decision. They needed to, for Lucie was very determined, and seldom did she fail to get her own way.

A Mr Benson was the manager of Bendicks chocolate establishment in Bond Street, and as well as selling chocolates also had a coffee house. He was a connoisseur of studio pottery, and a collector of work by Bernard Leach, Norah Braden and others. In his window, Mr Benson displayed Bendicks chocolates in ceramic bowls, which seemed to enhance the qualities of both. Lucie got an order to make pottery for the shop and this proved to be a lucrative commission. Coffee cups and saucers were needed, as well as little kidney-shaped side plates for biscuits. Lucie made cups without footrings, influenced by Bernard Leach, fired them to earthenware temperatures, and glazed them all in green and yellow. She hated them, but they kept on getting broken, and she had to make more and more. Very few are left now, and Lucie would certainly not want them illustrated in this book.

However, another pot from this period, when Hans Coper was working alongside her in Albion Mews, is the beautiful earthenware bowl with wide pulled lip illustrated on page 90. It carries low on its side the seal designed for her by Stanley North, and alongside an early and very rare seal for Hans Coper, indicating that in all probability Hans was responsible for the throwing. Soon Hans was to redesign both their seals, and made up numerous examples in different sizes for himself and for Lucie. The familiar seal which is shown on the half-title of this book and is regarded as a bench mark of quality is Lucie's seal, but its designer was Hans.

Lucie's Viennese friend Fritz Lampl was a regular visitor to the pottery and was liked by all, though he did not work there. He was still pursuing his glass-blowing business and some of the fine work he produced is shown on page 46. He would bring Lucie flowers on his weekly visits, and encouraged her when she was depressed just as he had in Vienna when he had displayed her work in his shop Bimini. Though Lucie denies it, he is remembered as having said, 'Lucie, you are a genius; one day you will be famous'. It was another wartime friend, Barbara Gomperts (no relation) who remembers this and how Lampl also saw a great future for Hans: 'He will be a great potter.'

By 1948 things were changing. Lucie and Hans together had evolved a range of tableware which owed nothing to tradition and was both functional and innovative. Salad bowls pulled at one side into a wide pouring lip were of such simple design that it is very hard to believe that they were without precedent.

Lucie packing the new stoneware kiln, 1948.

A salad bowl with a wide pulled lip.

The buttons had almost run their course and Lucie, having experimented with earthenware to its limit, was eager to try stoneware and emulate Leach with his high-fired ash glazes. She ordered a high temperature kiln – a major investment – and this bulky kiln which still occupies a quarter of her workshop was installed with help from Hans Coper. Being an electric kiln it would not quite reach the temperature needed for most of the Leach glazes in his *A Potter's Book*, which require 1300°C (cone 10), so improvization and experiment were necessary from the start. It is not difficult to imagine the excitement about the pottery as this massive piece of equipment started grudgingly to produce results. But Lucie, in the winter of 1948–49, decided to go on a skiing holiday to Switzerland by herself, and while she was away Hans and Jupp Dernbach tried a clandestine firing in the new kiln, over-firing everything and ruining their own pots.

Lucie wasted no time in modifying Leach's glazes to suit the temperature she had available. She modified all glazes to vitrify at 1260°C and has never wavered from this. She added lead to a Leach recipe for black glaze and produced a surface with a soft velvety sheen which served an assortment of lidded vessels for the table, and she used it and tin-based white glazes for other tableware, including teapots. The old plaited-cane handles she had used in Vienna for her teapots in conjunction with Ernst Plischke (see page 81) were replaced by bamboo-cane-handled teapots, using the traditional oriental design she had seen in the Leach pottery, and getting the handles made for her by a Japanese friend.

A Lucie Rie teapot, between two of the products of the Leach Pottery, c.1950

Hans Coper encouraged her to return to her pre-war concept of modern pottery, and as her work started to get lighter again she could hardly wait to prepare porcelain clay which could be fired in her new kiln, so the earliest Lucie Rie porcelain dates from 1949.

Through the Viennese circle of friends she was led to a Mr. William Ohly, who had opened the Berkeley Gallery in Mayfair, and in this year he asked Lucie if she would like to stage an exhibition. It was to be the first of several one-man shows at his gallery and the first time that she had put stoneware and porcelain before the public. There is no extant photograph of the exhibition, but many of the pots were hybrids, and one massive pot was produced at Mr Ohly's request as a centre-piece. It is the lidded jar shown on page 96, 36cm high and now in the collection of Sir David Attenborough.

In the late 1940s Lucie had a diverse circle of friends, and they included the historian Sir Louis Namier, originally from Poland, and the nuclear physicist Erwin Schroedinger, originally from Austria but based in Dublin, from where he conducted a lively correspondence with Lucie. Another influential friend was the New York photographer Stella Snead, who made regular visits to London and did her best to winkle Lucie out of Albion Mews and into the English countryside. Lucie went with the Ernst Freuds to Suffolk and with Bertl Saxl to Surrey, but with Stella Snead she set off by car to visit the prehistoric monuments at Stonehenge and Avebury. At the latter site, in the tiny museum, she saw some bronze age pottery bearing incised patterns, and alongside the exhibit were bird bones which appeared to have been the incising tools.

Sgraffito is a traditional method of pottery decoration which Lucie could have encountered and adopted at any time, but it was the dark bowls of Avebury which fired her enthusiasm and as soon as she came back to London she tried this technique, substituting a steel needle for the bird's bone. She used the needle to scratch patterns through layers of manganese oxide, and Hans Coper, without having seen the Avebury originals, used a similar technique in a much bolder way on the shallow bowls he was making in her pottery. Much of the pottery produced in Albion Mews at this time was chocolate brown and white. Tableware was matt brown to black outside, glossy white tin glazed inside, and the photographs right and on pages 114–15 show it well. The characteristic straight handles on coffee pots and jugs date from this time, and the newly learned sgraffito technique was used to lighten the forms.

In 1950 Lucie was to mount an exhibition at the Berkeley Gallery again, and this time Hans Coper shared the exhibition with her. In 1951 came the Festival of Britain. The Director General was Sir Gerald Barry, who lived in Albion Mews. He must have been aware of the creative activity on his doorstep, and Hans and Lucie were two of the potters whose work was included in this giant display devoted to contemporary rather than traditional design. In the same year Lucie and Hans were chosen as the only representatives of British ceramics at the Milan Triennale, where Lucie had been a gold medal winner in 1936. Another exhibition at the Berkeley Gallery was staged the same autumn, opened by the critic Maurice Collis. The pace of events was quickening. Lucie had photographs taken of her designs – mainly the sets of tableware – to assist her in marketing,

Bernard Leach's black stoneware glaze, modified and silky on a morning tea set made in 1950.

and Heal's in Tottenham Court Road started to stock her pots. Photographs of her work appeared in architectural magazines, where that affinity between her simple pots and modern 'baukunst', which had so intrigued Ernst Plischke, was evident again. Architects such as Ove Arup sought out her work at Heal's and bought. George Wingfield Digby, whose book *The Work of the Modern Potter in England* was published in 1952, included four full pages of photographs of her work, and a Lucie Rie teapot alongside teapots from the Leach pottery in St Ives.

Large stoneware pot, c.1950.

Early sgraffito tableware, chocolate brown outside, shiny white inside, familiar to the visitors to the pottery department of Heal's in the 1950s.

Lucie Rie pots in the bottom left-hand corner of a display at the Milan Triennale, 1951.

45

The Spanish potter Artigas (far left) photographed with Bernard Leach and Lucie at the Dartington Conference in 1952.

Lucie was invited by Bernard Leach to the International Conference of Craftsmen at Dartington Hall in July 1952 and she took Hans Coper with her, both of them displaying their work in the accompanying exhibition. Practically everyone in the English-speaking world concerned with crafts was there, plus a good few Japanese, and Lucie met Yanagi and Hamada.

Shoji Hamada's place as the greatest potter of the century was pretty well understood at this time, and Lucie naturally felt a respect for his work and his well integrated life, but she was not used to Japanese ways and found his subsequent visits to Albion Mews somewhat chauvinist. He and his friends would stay overnight and re-arrange Lucie's furniture to make it more aesthetically pleasing. Lucie changed it back again after they left. But as the years went by she came to appreciate and even feel an affection for this great man who found it hard to believe that a woman could have the necessary talents to be a fine potter.

With new-found confidence, a range of tableware which was quite unique, and the pleasure of working with the like-minded Hans Coper, Lucie exhibited again in 1952 at the Berkeley Gallery with Hans, and this time the show was opened by Ove Arup, who made a long speech encouraging everyone to buy. Things were going well. Another early supporter and champion of her work was Henry Rothschild, who had exhibited Lucie Rie pots in his Primavera Gallery in Sloane Street from the time that it opened in the late 1940s. He assisted in the assembly of an English ceramics exhibition at the Stedelijk Museum in Amsterdam in 1953, and Rie and Coper pots were included.

Amongst the happiest occasions during the early 1950s were the visits Lucie made to the home of Fritz Lampl in Hampstead. Other people from Albion Mews would go there, including Jupp Dernbach and Hans. Lucie's friend Barbara Gomperts remembers how animated Lucie and Fritz were when together.

46

Massive stoneware and delicate porcelain by Lucie Rie, arranged in the showroom of Bonniers, New York, 1954.

She would listen to him talking, about poetry and the theatre, and Lucie was never happier than when in his company. Every decade or so seemed to bring with it due measure of sadness for Lucie, because of the loss of someone central to her life, and when Fritz Lampl died of a heart attack after a short illness in 1954, Lucie was much cast down.

In the world of pottery, from the late 1940s on, Lucie is associated always with Hans Coper, but he was a workmate and colleague, and Fritz's death left a space in her life which was difficult for anyone to fill. She concentrated on exhibitions including the Milan Triennale, where she repeated her 1936 performance by winning another gold medal, and showed at the new ceramics gallery in the North of England, the Midland Group. She went to New York, where Mr Holmquist

of the House of Bonnier had commissioned a complete display of her tableware. This was a major breakthrough. Bernard Leach was lecturing in America about this time, but for a prestigious New York gallery to focus on Lucie Rie was a step towards world recognition, and she prepared a wide range of work, as shown in the photograph above.

The show at Bonniers was a great success – none of the pots came back to England – and Lucie took the opportunity of meeting up with emigré relatives and also with Hans Rie during her stay. There was another exhibition at the Berkeley Galleries shared with Hans Coper the same year, and a joint exhibition in Gothenburg in 1955.

By now, Bernard Leach was on the point of marrying again, this time to the Texan sculptress Janet Darnell, but before he did this, he went on holiday with Lucie and her friend Barbara Gomperts to Pembrokeshire in South Wales. With her concentration on her pottery, and long hours of work, the occasional breaks away from Albion Mews tend to stand out, and the sea bathing in Barafundle Bay while Bernard sketched wildlife and flowers on the sand dunes is a clear memory from the period. Bernard Leach was still cautious in his reaction to the modern and dynamic pots which were flowing from the pottery in Albion Mews, more particularly those of Hans Coper, and he could no doubt see the influence that this young man was having on Lucie's work, where his own influence had been stultifying. Lucie at this time, like Hans, made many experiments with composite forms and she placed

Fritz Lampl, poet, playwright, artist and friend. The spectacular glass, left, shows his great skill as glassblower and designer. Coll. Barbara Gomperts.

Long-necked vases – composite vessels decorated with sgraffito in the 1950s.

paired dishes on edge, and added to them long crane-like necks. Hans' new companion Jane Gate came to photograph them and they are well recorded above and on pages 148–9.

I suppose it is not surprising that Bernard's third wife Janet should have wondered about the ambivalent relationship between her husband and Lucie, with Bernard's need to seek her company and advice every now and then, and it is a tribute to the warmheartedness of both women that from their early meetings respect turned into friendship, Janet in due time becoming one of Lucie's most vociferous supporters. To begin with, however, they must have made a strange trio, the Texan, the Austrian and the Englishman, in the narrow streets of St Ives where Lucie, when she came to stay, was obliged to board in nearby lodgings. Bernard was a great talker, and would hold forth on practically any subject, and Lucie would listen.

It was about this time that Lucie made a move towards cooperation with industry. Looking back from the 1980s, it is easy to see how in recent years the positive design policy of certain mass market retailers such as Habitat have hugely influenced popular taste, just as Heal's and Liberty's did to a more elite clientele

in the period up to the Second World War. As arbiters of public taste, such companies have been able to re-shape industrial ranges of ceramics by commissioning them in quantity. There is, however, a significant gap over a period of about a quarter of a century (a period which includes the influential Festival of Britain in 1951), when manufacturers dictated public taste and, without feedback or perhaps ignoring feedback from the point of sale, standards declined and the industry, over-reliant on traditional designs, floundered.

At the far end of Europe, in Finland, the Arabia studio was employing artist designers to great effect, and in other Scandinavian countries, designer- rather than market-conditioned ceramics were setting a new, sleek if somewhat soulless style of tableware. In England at this time, and by the famous firm of Wedgwood, a fantastic opportunity was missed. Encouraged by Sir Paul (now Lord) Reilly, and before they adopted a policy of taking on art school graduates as studio potters in residence, the London director of Wedgwood approached Lucie Rie in Albion Mews for a range of tableware. She spent a rather uneasy day with the Wedgwood design team visiting the factory, and finally agreed in characteristic way to 'do her best'. Traditional Jasperware clays, blue and white, were provided by the company, with a brief to the potter to design and produce prototypes for tea and coffee sets. Hans Coper was probably much consulted, but the prototypes which emerged are Lucie's own. Combining attention to detail with economical functional form, and using a modified inlay technique which marries her sgraffito style with Wedgwood traditional practice, she produced the beautiful range of pots shown on the facing page.

The London director, Robin Riley, was delighted with them, and they went, wrapped in orange tissue paper, to Barlaston. It is certain that technical problems connected with the streaky white inlay could have

Jasperware cups and saucers designed for Wedgwood.

been overcome, but this may not even have been discussed by the company. The sales director was overruled, and Lucie was told that the pots were not suitable; that it was best if, in this case, designer and manufacturer went their separate ways. Maitland Wright, then managing director of Wedgwood, somehow indicated to Lucie that she was 'not a Wedgwood person.' Lucie was offered £29 for her time and effort, and she decided that she would rather have the prototypes back instead of this fee.

It is hard to know exactly how she took this news. I believe that a Wedgwood launch of these designs could have set English industrial pottery at the end of the 1950s off in a new direction with far-reaching effect, and perhaps the potter thinks so too. Certainly she is philosophical about the matter now, but it was the first and last time she tried any industrial cooperation, and her experience was even more stultifying than that of Hans Coper with regard to the acoustic and decorative bricks he designed, for they were at least manufactured for a few years. Hans took a more thoughtful view of the way in which the presentation of her designs had been organized. He told Lucie that she should have waited until she had designed the

coffee pots and teapots, and presented them to Wedgwood all together. Unfortunately the result of all this was that no Jasperware teapots and coffee pots were ever made by Lucie.

By the end of 1958, Hans Coper had moved out of Albion Mews, taking advantage of the offer of a studio in Hertfordshire to establish his own workshop. His move brought to an end the very close working relationship which had lasted for thirteen years, and during this time their very different pots had shown a certain family resemblance. The domestic ware was really a combined effort, Hans making a great many of the cups and saucers, and Lucie making the teapots and jugs: collectors look today with eagerness for the double seals which were stamped on the bottom of the jointly-made ware. Space in Albion Mews is very limited, and even when the button-making workforce had been reduced to just Lucie and Hans by about 1950, there was still barely enough space for two potters, and Hans wanted to make big pots. So he moved to Digswell, near Welwyn Garden City, and in 1969 Lucie got a car, which made visiting Hans in Hertfordshire easier.

49

Inlay ware in the Berkeley Gallery exhibition of 1960.

In 1960, Lucie had an exhibition on her own at the Berkeley Gallery, and was called again in the same year to exhibit in Holland. George Digby's enthusiasm for English contemporary pottery had excited the visiting Director of the Boymans Museum, Rotterdam, and Digby and Muriel Rose together were asked to choose the exhibits for what was to be a major incursion into Europe by English-based potters. Lucie took her participation very seriously, and the success of her and Hans' contribution meant that several Dutch students promptly came to England to find out what they could learn from Lucie and Hans at first hand.

Another chapter of Lucie's life began when she agreed to be a teacher at the Camberwell School of Art. Bernard Leach felt that it was time that Lucie shared her pottery knowledge and experience with others, or so he said in a letter to her which encouraged her to accept a part-time teaching position at Camberwell. Bernard Leach's son-in-law, Dick Kendall, was in charge of ceramics there, and a new diploma course promoted by the Ministry of Education was just starting, which allowed selected colleges to award their own qualifications. Art schools were vying with each other to present their own courses, and a prospectus with Lucie Rie's name on the staff list had a special cachet. This shows how her reputation had grown in her fifteen years of potting and exhibiting in Britain.

Lucie started to teach one and a half days a week, and after a year Hans joined her on the same basis, though their teaching days did not always coincide. She was to teach domestic pottery – 'teapots for discipline' – and gave demonstrations of throwing. Hans was to teach industrial ceramics, but soon both of them found that seminar-style teaching, or better still, tutorials with individual students suited them better. Hans was a marvellous teacher, able to understand his pupils, and give them as individuals real confidence, 'teaching from within'. Lucie was not a good teacher, unable to get into the mood of the school, and unwilling to bend herself towards unmotivated students. Of course to begin with the students were impressed by her very presence in the building, but later in the 1960s, as ceramics became less functional and the fashion turned to decorative techniques such as silk screening, about which she knew nothing, she rather lost heart.

Naturally, there were students, such as John Ward, Ian Godfrey and Ewan Henderson, who owe a good deal to Lucie, and some memorable occasions, such as the day when Lucie, Hans, Bernard Leach and Hamada were all there together, and Hamada gave a demonstration of throwing, sitting cross-legged on a pile of drawing boards, to bring him to the correct Japanese height for the wheel. He gave monosyllabic comments in Japanese which Bernard Leach translated into long English sentences, and Hamada made vases and 'fish-traps' with consummate ease, giving instructions before he left as to how they were to be glazed. The school followed his instructions, and the students appropriated the pots as mementoes.

Lucie as a teacher 'tried not to be negative without being too positive', and I suppose it was the rigorous standards which she applied which left some students in tears. Hans described her as a steel fist inside a suede glove, but she had come up against a generation of students who did not really want to be told that they would have to work hard for years and years. 'One day you will be a good potter,' was a dictum which Lucie relied upon perhaps too heavily. Her colleague at this time, Dennis Healing, remembers the embarrassment and difficulty when Lucie was involved in the selection of work for an end-of-year student exhibition, and rejected all the pots one after another, until the prospect of having an exhibition at all seemed to disappear. Lucie was also on the selection committee of the Design Council during the 1960s, and had the upsetting experience of rejecting, in all ignorance of its identity, work by her distinguished contemporary Michael Cardew.

Lucie was involved as a visiting lecturer at the Bristol School of Art, to which she made termly visits for a year or two, and a few times to the Royal College of Art where she came as Lord Queensberry's guest, and where she was given an Honorary Doctorate before the end of the decade. She finally give up teaching in 1972.

With some misgivings about sending her work to Germany, she exhibited at the international exhibition in Munich in 1964, and won a gold medal, and in the same year she was included in the international ceramics exhibition in Tokyo. Her work had now travelled all around the world, and museums and galleries as far apart as Melbourne and Minneapolis had bought pots for their permanent collections.

In 1965 Edwin Mullins put together an interesting selection of potters in a thoughtful exhibition in London at the Molton Gallery in South Molton Street, and Lucie's work was included. The Berkeley Gallery of William Ohly was rather a specialized gallery, concentrating in the main on the three-dimensional art of primitive peoples, and the small but discerning Molton Gallery

Above: Drawing of Lucie by Hans Coper. The original is in white chalk on dark grey paper.

Three pots from the 1962 exhibition at the Berkeley Gallery. They fit well into the ethnic environment.

51

was undertaking something new, at least in England, by exhibiting pottery, when 'fine arts' galleries normally only exhibited paintings and sculpture.

In the following year, 1966, John Sparks' gallery in Mount Street, noted for oriental works of art, particularly Chinese, decided to stage a modern pottery exhibition, bracketing together Swedish and English potters on the somewhat questionable thesis that these were the two countries which had best integrated the impact of Sung pottery into their contemporary ceramics. In the company of five Swedish potters were Bernard Leach, Alan Spencer-Green and Lucie Rie.

The whole exhibition was rather low-key, a harmonious exhibition rather than a dynamic one, with the emphasis on glazes which related back to oriental precedent. The catalogue declared that the modern potter needed to be painter, sculptor, draughtsman, chemist, physicist and craftsman; implying that crude and rugged native talent somehow had to be eschewed, or at least sublimated, and that the gallery was concerned to promote 'educated' ceramics. That Lucie's work should have fitted so well into this brief indicates not a readiness on her part to nod the head towards oriental inspiration, but simply that hers *is* educated pottery, which is at home in any company and holds its own with dignity. Of the forty-three pots which she exhibited, thirty-three were bowls, and in their Sparks context, many of her admirers who had always said of her work 'how modern', suddenly found that they were thinking 'how Chinese'. Lucie does not copy anybody. It is a sign of her greatness that one recognizes in her work other cultures, even artefacts in other materials, without her own original pots being diminished by the comparison.

Towards the end of 1966, the Boymans Museum in Rotterdam indicated that it would like to stage a one-man exhibition for Lucie, but Lucie said, 'Not without Hans,' and the most important joint exhibition of their career was planned to take place in 1967. Hans had by this time returned to London from Hertfordshire and made his pots for the exhibition from his new studio in Hammersmith. Lucie produced over a hundred fresh pots in a few months in Albion Mews. It was a frantic year, with another exhibition in Nottingham at the Midland Group, and a contribution to the *International Ceramics* in Istanbul.

But the time had come for an official tribute to Lucie's artistry and her hard work back at home. Alan Bowness, now Director of the Tate Gallery but at that time working for the Arts Council, proposed that a retrospective exhibition of her work be presented in London. The offer was an important one for Lucie, but the timing was difficult. The show in Holland was to be in spring 1967, and would travel to the Gemeentemuseum in Arnhem, taking with it all her latest work, which would thus not be available for London. All the same, Lucie agreed.

One of the Lucie Rie rooms at the Boymans Museum exhibition of 1967.

Cylindrical stoneware vase with white glaze on a dark blue body, made in 1960 and exhibited at the Arts Council exhibition. 11.5 cm high.

6
The Arts Council Exhibition

And so, at an age when men in Britain become old-age pensioners, Lucie was given the accolade of a one-man exhibition by the Arts Council. It was held in the elegant premises of the Arts Council itself, No. 4 St James's Square. Lucie, having potted for over forty years, nearly thirty of them in Britain, was in mid career with much of her best work still to come.

Bernard Leach gave his studied approval to this exhibition. Lucie in typical fashion had asked his opinion. 'Should I? Shouldn't I?', and Bernard wrote, Malvolio-like, 'Though one should not seek honours, one should graciously accept if they are thrust upon one.' He also wrote a brief introduction to the catalogue, wordy but unenlightening. By contrast, the main text of the catalogue, by the exhibition's own organizer, George Wingfield Digby, sensitively assesses the influence of Lucie's past on her current work, and places her in the context of craftsmen internationally, both in ceramics and other media. It is in his article in the catalogue that his much quoted description of Lucie is made, 'Here was a studio potter whose work was not rustic but metropolitan.' He was actually describing her work of the 1950s as exhibited in New York. He continued, 'Her work had no nostalgic undertones of folk art, the style was that of someone conscious of modern architecture.'

It was fortunate that George Wingfield Digby, of the Victoria & Albert Museum, was responsible with his wife Nelly for organizing and choosing the exhibits for the Arts Council exhibition. The arrangement of over three hundred and fifty pieces, well spread out in the gallery, was magnificent. The overriding impression given by this exhibition was of modernity and appropriateness for modern living, rather than work redolent of and nostalgic for the past and other cultures. George Digby seizes on this modernity in comparing her work favourably with that of the typical industrial designer of the time, a designer who never gets his fingers into the clay. He urges the viewer to feel the difference by picking up and holding a Lucie Rie pot, 'where the body and glaze are always integrated, and where the preparation and mixture of the body, be it stoneware or porcelain, is a highly individual matter . . . where results are always somewhat fugitive, uncertain, but then sometimes emerges from the kiln a pot which is a thing apart. . . .'

The exhibition travelled from London to Nottingham in August, and then to Bristol in October. In 1968, Lucie was given the OBE. She remembers her first visit to Buckingham Palace without any pleasure. Though no stranger to grand places, Lucie found both the building and the people who lined its corridors lofty, and was disappointed that the Queen herself seemed to have no interest in pottery. 'I don't know why they invited me', she said, 'I sat for hours; I had no-one to talk to, no interesting conversations.' But the conferring of the OBE was the moment of establishment recognition.

The importance of the Arts Council exhibition in helping those who knew of Lucie Rie, but associated her with chocolate-and-white tableware, to understand the breadth of her work and her comprehensive grasp of the nature of pottery, was immense. In a way that no commercial gallery showing new work could do, the Arts Council galleries unfolded her career stage by stage. One tenth of the exhibition was devoted to her Viennese work, another tenth to tableware, and in this exhibition, for the one and only time, was something made by Lucie which strictly speaking was not really a pot at all. It was a table, designed by Lucie, and made for the collector of her work, Cyril Frankel, in 1961. It consists of sixteen rectangular firebricks, glazed with differing cream, white and grey glazes, and mounted in a brass frame by Vilmo Gisello. The table, in its

Lucie Rie table in frame by Vilmo Gisello, 1961.

present setting, is shown below left. The combination of glazes, some crackled, is extremely subtle, and the whole design reflects the training of Hoffmann in Vienna, and perhaps of Plischke.

Muriel Rose, writing of the Arts Council exhibition, said: 'In England her understanding of design for present-day living at its most discriminating has brought her a devoted clientele and a unique place amongst the potters. . . . The range of work in the exhibition, both in scale and style, was a revelation even to those who had followed her development. . . . It emphasized her growing ability to decorate the form of her pots without losing their essential simplicity, and left no doubt of Lucie Rie's status as a leader amongst twentieth-century potters.'

In referring to her 'growing ability to decorate', Muriel Rose had certainly taken note of the spiral designs which Lucie had introduced by throwing with two-coloured clays, an important technique developed in 1967 which is described on page 68. In mentioning 'living at its most discriminating', Miss Rose is making an approving reference to the good manners of Lucie's pottery, its well-bred and well-groomed look. This parallels a comment made by so many of those who know Lucie as a person: that she has perfect taste in all things. Twenty years later, it has become almost necessary to apologise for having good taste, as so much of what is exhibited is aggressively vulgar. Interior design has gone through one if not two revolutions, and good taste and elitism have become almost synonymous. It would be fair to describe Lucie as elitist in the most favourable sense of the word: she certainly strives for the best, and admires the same in others. The inevitable rise in the prices of her work has confined it, unfortunately, to a small group, but Lucie has not ever deliberately restricted her output or prevented its dissemination as widely as possible. Jane Coper says that at one period she would adjust her prices when people came to her pottery to choose – and would disappear into a dark corner of her workshop to consult her 'price list', which was any handy book such as the telephone directory.

Letters written to Lucie by Ernst Plischke from New Zealand include one in which he described his own architectural work as 'a fight against vulgarity and ugliness, and a fight for cleanliness and order rather than for real beauty.' I suspect that he was dodging the problem of defining beauty, at least in relation to his own work, but much of what he wrote could apply to Lucie too. Though she is creating from a ball

Vase with inlay and sgraffito decoration through manganese, 23 cm high, c. 1960. Coll. J. Pike.

One of Lucie's favourite and most characteristic techniques first appeared in 1967: the integral coloured spiral design. The small pot on the left is oval, and 15.3 cm high. Both it and its neighbour, 27.5 cm high, are coloured green through a white porcelain glaze by copper carbonate in the spiral. The squared-off pot, right, is dark stoneware made of red clay and 'T' material, with manganese in the darker spiral. Dolomite glaze. 27.8 cm high, 1967.

*Lucie and Hans Coper in Somerset,
photographed by Stella Snead.*

of clay, her mental approach is similar to the subtractive technique of a sculptor, who cuts away and away. Perhaps it is not too far-fetched to remember in this context that Lucie's favourite process within the techniques of pottery making is turning (see page 66), which gives her the opportunity of rejecting the coarse and uncontrolled.

Her work has always, since 1946, borne some resemblance to that of Hans Coper, sometimes directly, and sometimes in reaction. His proximity in Albion Mews brought their work closer together, his departure drew forth from Lucie new ideas, new shapes, in compensation.

In mid 1967, Hans Coper moved out of London again, this time to Somerset. Instead of seeing Hans practically every day, either in Albion Mews or at his London studio only a few minutes away, she saw him only on his teaching days at the Royal College, and when they went to teach together at Camberwell School of Art. She now made visits to his home in Frome, and took an interest in the house which Hans was converting and the garden – a wilderness which she tackled with the fortitude one often recognizes in elderly women gardeners. The visits to Frome were happy ones, as shown above by one of many photographs taken there by her New Yorker friend Stella Snead.

For both Hans and Lucie, the early 1970s were years of greater stability, and were distinguished from previous decades because of the absence of financial pressures. Lucie was, after 1967, able to command her own prices, though the opportunities for exhibiting changed with the death of William Ohly, the closure of the Berkeley Gallery, and also the decamping of Primavera from London to Cambridge. There was no

obvious gallery in London where Lucie could hold one-man shows, though the appearance of the Marjorie Parr gallery in Chelsea gave her the opportunity now and then of exhibiting her work in mixed shows. To some extent it no longer really mattered; the pressure was off, and Lucie could find outlets for whatever she could produce, though she made special efforts for certain occasions. The Kettle's Yard exhibitions in Cambridge organized by Henry Rothschild from 1971 were amongst these, and there were contributions to exhibitions in Copenhagen, Osaka, Kyoto, Dusseldorf, and, with Hans Coper, a two-man show in Hamburg in 1974. In fact, detailing all the exhibitions to which she contributed in this fruitful decade would be tedious and difficult, since there were so many, but this indicates the professionalism of a potter who was aware that to disappear from the public view was to disappear from notice.

Many superb pots from the period are illustrated in the picture section of this book, and the fact that pots of this time cluster more densely on the pages indicates that the author, at least, regards them as her most important works. Not many people, even creative artists, are at their peak in their seventies.

By 1975, an illness which had struck Hans Coper was diagnosed as Motor Neurone Disease, for which there is no cure and no respite. Lucie, who had experienced the death of so many men close to her, felt the chill of another impending loss, and her visits to Hans and Jane Coper in Frome became a more painful delight, and more of a pilgrimage. Lucie's great pleasures in life apart from her work have been her interest in and concern for certain other people, to whom she is tenaciously devoted. Most artists of her stature enjoy or at least acknowledge the value of artistic endeavour in other fields, but for Lucie, music, literature, poetry, theatre and opera have never had much meaning. She has endured them for the sake of her friends from time to time; even visual and graphic arts are of only limited interest. Nothing really matters to her outside her work apart from certain friends and friendships. Over thirty years of friendship with Hans Coper took precedence, by 1975, over everything else. The progression of his illness, and what she might do to alleviate it, dominated her thoughts.

Bernard Leach, approaching ninety, and commemorated by an exhibition of his work at the Victoria & Albert Museum in 1977, was still a part of her life, though his restless energy was exhausting, and the blindness which had caused him to stop potting about this time increased the need for conversation. Lucie's visits to Hans in Frome had eclipsed the journeys to St Ives, and as Bernard became less mobile, their contact was weakened. A 'sgraffito' birthday cake had once been made for him with her customary skill and care, and personal gifts of great importance passed from Lucie to Bernard, but they met very little.

In 1979, as Lucie was preparing for an exhibition in Dusseldorf, she heard that Bernard, now 92, was seriously ill and asking to see her. She telephoned Janet in preparation for a visit to St Ives only to be told of his death that morning, and having failed to see him again in life, she decided not to go to his funeral. With the unemotional logic of the agnostic, she could see no point in attending a mere ritual, and in any event she had had in her life a great many funerals to attend.

An inexhaustible subject of delight: Bernard Leach discusses the merits of a pot with Lucie, 1970s.

7 A Chapter of Techniques

Vienna 1930

Old photographs of Lucie at work in her Wollzeile studio in Vienna show nothing unusual in her technique or her products. The background is tidy – amazingly so for a pottery – and the pots look ordinary enough. Lucie was concentrating on shapes which pleased her; her Viennese teapots and coffee pots were not very practical. They had throwing lines which showed their wheel-thrown origin, but these were left on for visual and tactile effect.

Dry sieving through a coarse lawn.

They were covered with unusual glazes of Lucie's own invention, in dark colours, including red, and relied on their glazed surfaces for their decoration. Lucie, unlike her Viennese contemporaries, never painted designs on her pots. In spite of her early talent for drawing she was reluctant to experiment even with linear patterns, and preferred her pots to depend for their effect on the marriage of form and glaze.

All the work from this time and up to 1948 was earthenware. With her talent for making the best of what the circumstances offer, and turning to advantage what others would find inhibiting, she halved the danger of damage to her work during the tram ride across Vienna to the nearest kiln by glazing her pots unfired, so that they only went once across the city, and has used the once-fired approach ever since. The importance of this to her work in general is enormous.

In the Albion Mews pottery a gas flame, like a gas poker but not under pressure, is always alight. It has the function, in her well organized studio, of drying the atmosphere to speed up the sequence of pottery making. Very absorbent firebricks, placed on a horizontal iron grille above it, are kept bone dry and warm, and nearly-dry pots are often stood on top of the bricks to complete the drying process. However, an important function of the dry bricks is in the preparation of clay from powdered ingredients. Porcelain clay, for instance, is made by mixing China clay, ball clay, felspar and Bentonite, sieving the ingredients dry first through a coarse '40' mesh sieve, and then ensuring an even consistency when water has been added. The same procedure, with fine sieving, is followed in making glazes, a fairly tedious process familiar to all potters. However, the preparation of *clay* in this liquid way requires some help in speeding up the drying so that the clay can be made plastic and workable. This is where the absorbent bricks come in, for Lucie wraps the creamy grey porcelain mix in a cotton cloth, and then arranges the bricks above and below, like a monster sandwich, allowing them to soak up the moisture. By this means she can make plastic porcelain clay from powder in one week or less.

On one side of the top-loading kiln is the kneading bench, where she prepares thirteen or more kilos of plastic clay at a time, and under the windows are the two continental-style wheels brought with her from Vienna, one her own and one from her cousin. They

The kneading bench.

differ from the typical English wheel in that the wheel-head stands high, rather than being surrounded by a high-rimmed container to catch water and waste clay; the only protection which the potter has is a canvas apron attached to the wheel assembly which comes up to cover the potter's knees. The photograph on the facing page clearly shows the layout, with tools within hand-reach on the board behind, and the bench on which the potter sits. Such a wheel soon teaches a potter not to use too much water, which would be flung off the wheel as well as creating a pool in the centre of the pot, a situation which Lucie deplores: 'If you use too much water, after two minutes you will not be throwing the pot, it will be throwing you.' The photograph shows how immaculately clean Lucie manages to keep her working area, but it does not show the massive wooden flywheel under the bench, which is the other characteristic of the continental design. Weighing perhaps forty kilos, it keeps the momentum going for a long time once it has been kicked round by the potter's foot, and well-engineered bearings make this easy work. Nevertheless, Lucie had one of her two wheels motorized in the 1960s to reduce the amount of footwork, and it is on this wheel, shown opposite, that she now does all her throwing.

Potters who watch her work on the wheel are interested to see the use she makes of a metal kidney – a simple tool, in her case made of copper and shaped like a comma – which replaces the fingers in making a smooth surface both on the inside and the outside of a bowl.

Centering the clay is the first process a thrower undertakes on the wheel, and Lucie wastes as little time on this as possible. After all these years she knows exactly how much a tall bowl-shape can be allowed to wobble before it faces collapse, and she is not much concerned as to whether or not a pot is running true in the engineering sense when it is in her hands on the wheel. For this reason many of her pots have unlevel rims, they dip down to one side, or stand slightly at an angle. Her intuitive sense tells her when a pot is 'right', and this has about as little to do with pure symmetry as have the petals of a rose.

Copyists of Lucie Rie who aimed to introduce an imitative wobble or 'quiver' into the work would end up with something ungainly, and those who do copy her flaring bowl shapes, but ensure that they are level at the top and precisely balanced, produce objects which are uninterestingly perfect.

The bowls start tall on the wheel, and widen as they progress. The outside profile of the finished bowl is never a simple curve, and may incorporate and accentuate the bellying form which other potters recognize as the moment before disaster, when the weight of the rim is too heavy for the walls. Lucie controls and freezes this form, as well as the even more difficult and flaring shape shown on page 97, to add to the dynamic effect, and this is often further enhanced if the rim rises and falls slightly, like a child's spinning top just before it topples to a stop.

Squeezing a bowl into an oval form will accentuate the undulation of the rim.

A chapter of techniques

Many of Lucie's thin-necked pots are made in two pieces, because it is not worth the struggle of containing and hoisting up enough clay to make a neck on a globular form, when two separately thrown pieces can be so easily joined. So Lucie will throw two rather ungainly pieces with her mind on the finished form, which comes from combining the shapes one on top of the other and joining them first with water and then with a thin sausage of clay, smoothing this in with the useful kidney tool, and a sponge.

Many potters would throw up their hands in horror at the use of sandpaper, believing that it dulls and deadens the surface of their pots, but Lucie has no such inhibitions, and when the pot is dry the join is sand-papered to her satisfaction. The pots shown right are made in this way, and many have also been heartily squeezed at the join for good measure.

Vases, each made from two pieces joined, sandpapered and left unsqueezed. White porcelain and mirror-black stoneware, 18 cm and 25 cm high, c.1962. Both coll. Charmian Young.

Putting two or more pieces together to make a harmonious whole can be extremely difficult, especially if the units are squeezed oval first. This pot, which Lucie has never been able to repeat, she keeps in her show-room. Stoneware, green-grey felspathic glaze, 20 cm high, c.1975.

The characteristic profile of a Lucie Rie bowl often depends on the narrow, deeply turned foot-ring.

The turned foot-ring of the bowl shown in colour on page 197. The typical design of radiating lines around the seal is scratched through red iron oxide.

Apart from the 'Bernard Leach period', when she was persuaded to leave the foot of her work as it came from the wheel (Leach's pots often show the lines of the cutting wire, and he disapproved of too much time spent on the process of tidying up the base known as 'turning') Lucie always takes care to ensure that the base of the pot is as well finished as the top. Indeed, many of the pots she decorates with detailed sgraffito, as well as the later 'knitted' pots of the 1970s, have immensely detailed designs scratched and sometimes painted on to the base after turning so that the examination of a Lucie Rie pot of this period is a revelation rather like examining the shell of a sea-urchin, or the markings on the body of an insect under a magnifying glass.

The reflex action which makes lovers of silver seek the expected marks on the base of a treasure applies also to Lucie Rie collectors, who anticipate and experience real pleasure from turning the pot up to look at its immaculately finished foot and seal. Of course there is a danger in over-concentrating on such details. Victor Margrie rather waspishly described Lucie as, 'making obvious shapes and then spending all her time scratching patterns on the bottom.' Lucie's recent work has less elaborately decorated feet, but always a very deep foot-ring which one cannot resist examining for the pleasure of it, as one might examine the dovetail joints in the drawers of a master cabinet-maker's chest.

65

A finished glazed pot is used to support a delicate pot for turning.

Shown here twice actual size, the LR on the seal projects as a fine ridge of clay in a shallow depression. Try to avoid the 'reversing effect' which makes it appear wrongly as a cushion with incised initials.

Lucie's turning tools are the metal kidney, a razor blade, and a piece of pallet-banding metal fashioned into a loop by Hans Coper. She does not use any of the standard heavy metal tools, with cutting edges at right angles to the shaft, and is not deterred by chatter-markings which appear on the surface of the pot because of the lightness of her tools: 'They will be covered by the glaze,' she says. The turning stage is the time when the foot-ring is made and the seal is put on. Originally made in Plaster of Paris, the seals were replaced with earthenware ones by Hans Coper, but Lucie did not like them so much and reverted to plaster. The incision in the seal is a fine one and the only way to get a sharp impression is to press soft clay from the turnings first into the seal itself, and then apply it to the pot: a technique which is rather like sprigging. The pot is then allowed to dry and is absolutely bone-dry before she applies colouring slip and glaze. The fact that Lucie cuts out completely the first, or 'biscuit', firing and proceeds to decorate and glaze an unfired pot has already been mentioned and is well known and vital to her work. It is a system avoided in industry and shunned by other studio potters, partly because of the hazards of handling an unfired pot. Thinly thrown ware is likely to warp or crack when subjected unfired to the shock of immersion in a bucket of glaze. The holding of a teapot by its handle, for instance, is simply not possible if the pot has not been into a kiln and become hard and permanent. But Lucie does not dip or pour when she is glazing – she *paints* glaze on, thickly, with a flat house-painter's brush as the pot revolves on the wheel. For those who find the mystique of painting with bamboo-handled brushes and liners rather daunting, it is reassuring that a long established master should use such a humble and minimal tool as a house-painter's brush, but the way in which Lucie applies the glaze, mixed with gum arabic to make sure that it sticks to the dry pottery surface and does not flake off, is extremely important. Most ceramic glazes, earthenware and stoneware, are applied with a consistency similar to thin cream. Lucie's glazes are rather thicker – almost as thick as yoghurt – and are applied to the clay first on the outside and then on the inside of the bowl or pot. For an obvious technical reason the sequence of coating one surface of a pot before the other normally means inequality in the thickness of the glaze outside and inside, because of the pot's absorbency, but not if one uses Lucie's method, which is to allow the half-glazed pot to sit for a time drying, and when she later paints the inside, to go on applying glaze until it is as thick as she likes. Her experience tells her exactly when to stop.

Many of Lucie's pots are glazed with more than one glaze, one painted on top of the other, permutations which give many possibilities for surface and colour. Much of the special quality of her work derives from her immense skill and experience in this respect.

Certain glaze faults, in particular 'crawling', are minimized by painting the glaze on, and Lucie is genuinely at a loss to understand why so many potters persist with what she calls the 'primitive' method of dipping and pouring, when her system is so obviously superior. For many of Lucie's pots, the glaze *is* the decoration. Any additional decoration, if it is not already in the pot in the form of a coloured spiral band in the body, will probably be a series of horizontal bands or a coat of manganese oxide, or perhaps a fine painting of manganese oxide with copper carbonate brushed on to the very rim itself (which has been sponged clean of glaze), but which later bleeds into the sides of the pot (see page 217).

If it is sgraffito or inlay design then this once again is where the sharp needle is her simple tool. Radiating lines, parallel lines at an angle to the form, and fine cross-hatching were characteristic of Lucie's pottery in the 1950s, especially the radiating lines coloured with oxide, which make the top of her pots look like lily flowers (see page 147). Later she combined cross-hatched sgraffito with heavy glazing in the so-called 'knitted' pots, pages 209–11. An extension of the technique produces a form of inlay in which the grooves scratched into the body are filled with colorants such as lead chromate painted on and then sponged off the unfired clay, leaving the colour only in the grooves (see page 119). The final colour of the inlay depends on whether or not there is a coat of glaze over all, and complex variations of texture and colour come from glazing the inlaid surface with different glazes.

Brushing on glaze

The sgraffito technique of scratching through manganese to the bare white porcelain (see pages 44–5) is one with which early collectors of Lucie Rie are familiar, and is well illustrated right and below, with its negative on the outide.

It should really be mentioned that the painstaking sgraffito technique with a needle is a long-winded business, like tattooing, and more than doubles the amount of time which a pot takes to make. Lucie's great skill in the fine-detailed sgraffito pots, which span the central part of her career from the late 1940s to the end of the 1960s, lies in matching the design with manganese of appropriate thickness; sometimes this rises up around the sgraffito design with an arched meniscus, and sometimes the manganese is so thin that it is like a varnish.

Done mechanically or clumsily, sgraffito can be a boring and soulless technique, like scraperboard; also, when applied to finely thrown porcelain, it can be an extremely dangerous technique as far as the structure of the pot is concerned, since the incising of the clay weakens the wall and sometimes, even with Lucie's

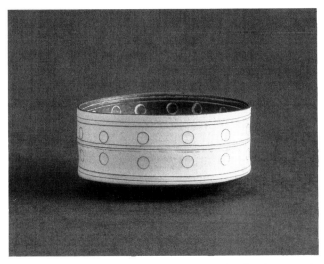

The circular incisions on this finely thrown porcelain bowl were made with the ferrule of a broken paint brush and were then inlaid with red iron slip. Inside the bowl the pattern is reversed with sgraffito through manganese. 11 cm diam., made before 1960.

experience, the pot will be lost when it bursts apart like a seedpod along one of the incised lines. Lucie's sgraffito design, sometimes making use of the revolving wheel to assist her, treads a delicate path between admirable precision and neatness on the one hand and boring repetitive accuracy on the other. The slight variation in the lines on the pots shown, for example, on pages 164–5, illustrates her use of sgraffito and inlay at its best, and her skill in the placing of the lines on the form as a whole.

It is some years since Lucie has used other tools for decoration, though in the past broken pens and the ferrules of paintbrushes have been called in to make circular decorations, or even deep holes punched through the fabric of the fine porcelain – 'Never use rice grains – they always make burrs.' Two examples are illustrated on page 95.

In early 1967 Lucie found a new basis for decoration as important in her career as the discovery of sgraffito at Avebury, and a great deal more personal. By throwing a pot from two balls of different coloured clays, pressed together but not 'mixed', a spiral pattern is made in the thrown pot, and this is particularly clear if the potter uses very little water in the throwing. It is given a different quality in the turning and again affected in the firing, especially if the glaze is a pale one, which will be coloured by the ingredients of the darker clay. Lucie remembers well the first pot she made using this

Inlaid and sgraffito lines carefully placed on the inside and outside of a porcelain bowl. 20.5 cm diam., c.1970. Fischer Fine Art.

Integral spiral stripes from throwing with unmixed clays of contrasting colour are evident in the flaring rim of this tall pot thrown in two parts. Stoneware, grey glaze, 38 cm, 1967. Victoria & Albert Museum.

technique (it is shown on page 57), but she is vague or reticent about its sources. It seems unlikely that such a simple device could have remained untried through centuries, but certainly Lucie was the first person to use it in Britain and was immediately copied by a whole generation of younger potters.

For darkened clay, Lucie uses either manganese $\left(1\frac{1}{2}\%\right)$, copper oxide $\left(0.25\%\right)$, cobalt $\left(1\%\right)$ or iron oxide $\left(3\%\right)$, and the metals in the clay affect the expansion and contraction rate when heat is applied, so that the 'first pot', referred to above, and other early examples are cracked. It was necessary to adjust the unaltered clay to match the oxided clay, and to make a better integrated and stronger body. Lucie did this by adding felspar to the white clay. Spiral-decoration pots and bowls proliferated in Albion Mews in the early 1970s and are much prized today by collectors. The process of dating Lucie's pots is full of pitfalls but at least with the spiral pattern examples, it is impossible for any of them to have been made before 1967.

The fluting of stoneware, often in a spiral around the body of the pot, is done when the pot is leather-hard

Spiral fluting carved on the body of a stoneware pot when leather hard: brown spots from manganese dioxide burn through a dolomite glaze. 19 cm, 1972.

69

with a spoon-shaped metal tool. On her tool there are scoops of different sizes, one at each end, but when Lucie is fluting the outside of a large bowl, for instance, and the increasing diameter of the bowl as she moves away from its centre dictates that each flute should widen towards the rim, the scoop is not wide enough, so Lucie has to carve the shape she wants by eye, with no reference to the width of the tool. Although very numerous in the 1950s and 60s, fluted pots are not so common in her current output.

Potters know how handles and spouts are applied and how pots are 'fettled' before firing, and for non-potters technical descriptions of these processes would be boring. For the technically minded however, some useful information may be found in the captions to the photographs of her work, pages 81–221. Lucie does not guard her recipes as trade secrets, but she knows, as all potters do, that it is one thing to have in front of one both the glaze recipe and the pot which has been decorated by it, quite another to be able to reproduce the same glaze results, however carefully one follows the formula. Her knowledge of chemistry completes the sparse repertoire of decorative aids in Lucie's workshop, if one excludes her own hands, which are often used to ease a thrown shape into an oval one, or to press a cylinder into a square. Without the wheel Lucie would be lost. With it she has no need of aid or other inspiration.

Keeping the bases of the pots clear of the kiln shelf when in the kiln by placing them on separately thrown rings of clay is a practice Lucie has adopted for many years. This, especially if the rings are painted with zirconium oxide, will stop any unexpectedly fluid glaze from glueing the pots permanently to the shelves. Although these rings are not as unstable as the tripod stilts used for earthenware, it is still a rather anxious business arranging a wide bowl with a small foot on an even smaller ring when it has to be done from above, and if a bowl or tall pot topples off its ring in the kiln it is likely to be distorted or to cause damage to pots alongside. It is therefore quite extraordinary (and amusing to Lucie) that after nearly forty years of such struggling she has only just hit on the idea of glueing the ring to the foot of the pot *before* putting it into the kiln, where of course the gum arabic burns away and the difficulties of kiln packing are halved.

Unfired clay, or 'greenware' as it is called, can be destroyed if any dampness remains in the clay at the time of firing. Lucie's pots have not only dried once but have been wet again by the glaze application, and nothing is packed in the kiln until it is absolutely bone dry.

The rise of temperature must be kept very carefully controlled, as chemically combined water in the clay can still crack pots apart if heating up is too rapid in the first half of the firing. The 28 kilowatt kiln of 1948 vintage will take up to twenty-two hours to reach stoneware temperatures, and the last hour of the firing is the most critical. Lucie does not 'soak' the ware in the kiln, as many potters do by keeping it at a chosen temperature for perhaps half an hour so that the heat accomplishes more, but instead turns the electricity off as soon as she sees through the spyhole that the Seger cone has bent over. Two spyholes are fitted, but Lucie's experience with this well-behaved kiln is such that she only uses a temperature check in the upper spyhole, relying on her eyes and on an ancient pair of Viennese sunglasses.

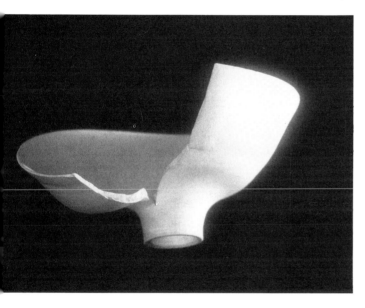

In all it is three days before the pots come out of the kiln, and for unpacking it is best to climb into the kiln and hand the cooled pots out to a helper. Dr Max Mayer is the regular helper now, though Lucie still climbs inside and hands the pots up. There are well-known photographs of Lucie's legs being held by Hans Coper and others to prevent her toppling in, and in the days when she had to tackle this alone she used to tie heavy weights to her ankles to hold her legs down. That she should have to go through this physical ordeal in her mid eighties is because the alternative (apart from handing over the whole business of firing to someone else) is a front-loading kiln, with heavy shelves that are difficult to position, and a great strain on the arms.

Kiln design has been revolutionized in the 1980s, but it does not seem likely that Lucie will change the arrangements she has used for half her life, or use any heat source other than electricity. In Vienna, kilns were coal-fired. In St Ives, following oriental practice, Bernard Leach used oil and wood (although Cornwall is a county almost treeless), and many potters of the present generation prefer the flames of direct heat – oil or gas – to electricity. Until fairly recently, and certainly while popular studio pottery was high-fired, it was felt that electricity gave dull results and that there was something bright-eyed about ware that came from the flames of burning gas, oil and wood. Lucie's success in producing an astonishing range of brilliant greens, pinks, yellows, and turquoise blues from the oxidizing atmosphere of an ordinary electric kiln is often cited to prove that electric kilns are as good as any. The truth is that Lucie's prodigious intuitive chemical knowledge gives her the ability to make the electric kiln give of its best.

The whole process of kiln firing is to create on the surface and into the body of the pot the very best visual, tactile, practical result from a combination of chemical materials. If it were easy, then Korean pottery, Persian pottery and European lead-glazed earthenware could be copied exactly and would not be revered for the skill of its makers. The integration of clay and glaze by the once-firing technique is Lucie's chosen route to aesthetic excellence. In some respects once-firing eases the path, but it has its own problems, and Lucie knows that success depends on endless experiment and familiarity with both kiln and materials.

Spectacular splitting in the kiln gives this porcelain pot an organic form. Though discarded by Lucie, it is now a treasured part of the collection of Cyril Frankel.

8 The early 1980s

In 1980, when nothing else in particular was happening, Lucie was taken by Sir Robert and Lisa Sainsbury to see the new Norman Foster building which had been completed at the University of East Anglia to house the Sainsbury Centre for Visual Arts, and the Sainsbury Collection. Ever interested in architecture, Lucie was impressed by the new direction in architecture which this rather severe building represented. In an un-premeditated flash of inspiration, Lady Sainsbury said, 'Would you like to have an exhibition of your work here?' And Lucie said, 'Yes . . . but I will have to square it with the V & A.'

A stoneware vase from the 'black firing' of 1981. 22 cm high. Coll. Cyril Frankel.

Sir Robert Sainsbury financed the assembling of a second retrospective exhibition – not as big as the Arts Council show of fourteen years earlier, but more expansive and, of course, much wider in range since it included the pots of the 1970s, which many regard as her best work. John and Carole Houston were called upon to organize the exhibition and its accompanying book, and the complex business of collecting and choosing pots in conjunction with Lucie began. Lucie worked hard to make new pots for the show.

In the middle of these preparations, Hans Coper died, wearied by his struggle against Motor Neurone Disease. Lucie had known for some time that there was no alternative; it was bound to happen, but the very best of all the men she had known in her life had gone. Lucie took marguerites, which reminded her of the happiest days on the Brunnerwiese in Eisenstadt, to the simple funeral in Bath. By a curious chance the next kiln firing at Albion Mews was over-fired, and the pots therein came out leaden black in colour, unlike anything else she had ever made and therefore linked forever with the date of mid 1981.

It would have been difficult for Hans had he lived to have visited the Sainsbury Centre near Norwich for the opening of the exhibition in November of that year, in view of his paralysis, but those who did attend and remember the opening by the then Minister for Arts, Paul Channon, will recall how sad and lonely Lucie seemed in that patrician gathering. The exhibition, however, was a brilliant success, the spacious arrangement, as in 1967, allowing the pots to express their modernity. It was later to move to the Victoria & Albert Museum in London, where the turnstiles whizzed round in an unprecedented way for an exhibition of work by a living potter. The Bernard Leach exhibition

Some of the showcases and, left, an aerial view of the Lucie Rie exhibition at the Sainsbury Centre for Visual Arts, University of East Anglia, 1981.

73

Part of the exhibition at Kunstkammer Köster, Mönchengladbach, 1978.

millions more people became aware overnight of the name and work of Lucie Rie in that year, when she also received her second honour from the Queen, the CBE.

The prices of her work rose quickly, and gallery prices of over £1000 for a single pot became common, yet a sort of hiatus descended after 1982, the year of her eightieth birthday, and the normal work pattern returned with few interruptions.

In November 1983 Peter Dingley mounted an exhibition of over fifty new pots at his gallery in Stratford-upon-Avon. Lucie was delighted with the way he displayed her work, and said that the gallery had allowed her to see her work properly for the first time. Certainly it was a memorable exhibition, with a new range of colours extending from peacock-blue and gold to sage green and magenta. What was extraordinary about the exhibition was that so few people attended. After all the hullabaloo in 1982 her first one-man exhibition in a commercial gallery in England for over twenty years was largely ignored – presumably because it was not in London. Lucie enjoys working for an exhibition and had worked extremely hard for the Stratford show. It represented quite a new phase in her work, a return to a brilliance and brightness of colours which recalled her Viennese pots, and even the buttons, but had been suppressed during the years of her association with Hans. Since every new glaze and every new shape had to pass the test of being shown to and approved of by Hans, his absence forced her to trust her own judgement in matters of colour and design, and a return to the rich

of 1977 had far fewer visitors, and it has to be admitted that television has something to do with this. Between the opening in Norwich and the opening in London the film-maker Cyril Frankel persuaded Lucie to agree to be filmed at work, and to talk about her pottery on film with David Attenborough, a long-time admirer and collector of her pots. The resulting film, only twenty minutes long and shown in the television *Omnibus* programme, is attractively informal and relaxed, quite a tribute to both the film-maker and David Attenborough, since Lucie has shunned a high public profile, and always avoided taking part in public events to do with crafts.

The film concentrates on her quest for excellence and her devotion to pottery, but is affectionately human in both the dialogue with David Attenborough, and the shots of Lucie perilously close to falling inside her own kiln. The power of television being so great,

The opening of the Hans Coper exhibition at the Sainsbury Centre for Visual Arts at Norwich, 1983.

and the jewel-like was the result. Those who saw this immensely important exhibition in Stratford saw a new potter emerging, as if sunlight suddenly illuminated a dark wood, and shone on multi-coloured flowers.

In the main the pots were rather smaller than in the past. At eighty-one, Lucie, for this exhibition, did not attempt to make massive stoneware pots, or to give the exhibition a centrepiece. Because of the small attendance, not all the pots were sold.

The next summer Lucie went on holiday to Spain, in company with and encouraged by Max Mayer and his wife Yvonne. She determined to exercise her body as in the old days, with walks, new sights and visits to museums. She was pressed to go to America where Hans Rie was in failing health, but resisted, and returned to her normal work pattern, fulfilling orders from private individuals and commercial galleries.

A healthy order book was no longer really relevant to Lucie's trading position, but it fulfilled important functions. She had for so long been insecure that it was a cushion and a reassurance, an indication of the world's continued interest in her activity, and also a tangible, practical reason for continuing to get up at 5.00 a.m. and to work through the day every day instead of retiring to slipperdom and reading from a chair. The scorn with which Lucie would regard such 'retirement' only reinforces what is familiar to all who know her: that she lives for her work and through her work. Cooking and cakemaking, marmalade-making and routine social engagements take their place, but work is the matrix into which everything else must somehow fit.

In 1985 Dr Max Mayer gave up his medical practice and started to work at the pottery, as a 'mature student'. Lucie welcomed this, and was soon describing him as the best student she had ever had. He was there to make his own pots, not to assist her, and soon she yielded to him her motorized wheel, though she agreed that he could help her with packing and unpacking the kiln. Her deliberations regarding buying a new and simpler kiln are unresolved, as long as Max or someone strong is there to help.

Shortly after the Stratford exhibition, Lucie participated in a two-man show at the Fischer Gallery in London. The gallery had bought in a large number of Hans Copers as well as several pots by Lucie, and she supplemented these with her new work. In 1985 some of her pots were exhibited in the Keramion in Frechen near Cologne, although this was part of a combined exhibition of English potters, organized by Henry

Max Mayer with Lucie in Albion Mews, 1987.

Rothschild, and did not contain pots which were specially made.

Another exhibition at the Fischer Gallery called 'nine potters' but effectively dominated by Lucie Rie, contained over seventy new pots, many of them massive stoneware, and a considerable physical achievement for a potter now in her eighty-fifth year. Lucie had enjoyed a second Mediterranean holiday with Max Mayer, this time in Cyprus, where she appreciated the bright colours of the Cyprus mountains and sky, dignified peasant architecture and good ceramic museums. A similar visit to Portugal in Spring 1986 was planned but had to be cancelled when she had a long bout of influenza. The death in the spring of her friend Theo Frankel, her original sponsor when she came to England before the war, a constant advisor through the post-war years and later on her 'finance minister', meant a conclusion to the Viennese connection, at least at the British end. One more friendship of half a century's standing had gone and perhaps Lucie made a conscious effort to take stock of those of her own generation who remained.

Never does one single week go by without a visitor or a call from America or Europe and regular telephone contact with both Janet Leach and Jane Coper revives her memories of the dead as well as the living.

Very few people failed to get on with Hans Coper, but one of them was Ernst Plischke, who had returned from New Zealand to Vienna in the 1960s as Professor of Architecture, directing his own school. After the death of Hans Coper and of his own wife Anna, Ernst Plischke was moved to rebuild his friendship with Lucie, who went to Vienna to visit him in 1983 for his eightieth birthday celebrations. It is a curious friendship, with both parties fiercely proud of the other's achievements in life, and Plischke came to England to see Lucie in 1985 and again in 1987. Now retired from architectural practice, it must be a satisfying experience for him to sit again in the much loved chairs he designed for her Wollzeile flat over sixty years ago, having in the intervening time built pioneering buildings on quite a different scale right across the world. And Ernst Plischke is undoubtedly one of the greatest admirers of her pots.

Professor Ernst Plischke

9 Last Chapter

Lucie says that she is 'just a potter', and that pots do not mean anything. It is a relief to find her so down-to-earth, for although it is the intellect of her friends which often draws her towards them, she is not an intellectual herself, and avoids any kind of philosophical discussion in relation to her work.

A newcomer meeting Lucie for the first time as she enters her eighty-sixth year would find her extremely courteous and correct, generous up to a point with her time, and if the meeting were in some way formal or official, extremely hospitable as regards coffee and home-made chocolate cake. Being so well-known has meant more invasion of her privacy than she would wish, although her constant need for the confirmation of friendships, and the visitors both social and business who are the embodiment of this, mean that she tolerates interruptions to her work routine which others of her age would not stand. The gap, however, between her courteous attitudes to visitors and her private assessment of people is often wide, and the façade she can erect is really Viennese. If she is interested in a visitor she will take pains to ask pointed questions which will reveal how much a person really knows or cares about pottery, and she has a merciless scorn for the deceitful. This has rather come to the fore in recent years, since the value of her pots has increased so spectacularly. Some collectors fail adequately to conceal from her their mercenary motives, yet even some of these people hold her affection and she gives them a helping hand.

Long-term friends and friendships are absolutely sacred. So many of the important men friends in her life have died that nearly all of her surviving 'old' friends are women, and without a family of her own, however famous she may be, she could be very lonely indeed if friendships were not nourished. As chit-chat about pottery and pottery trends tends to bore her, and her friends anyway come from a variety of professions, she is more interested in what other people are doing, and applauds success. If success means working hard and overcoming obstacles, then whether it is in the Bolshoi or in the motor trade is irrelevant to her. A concomitant impatience with failure depends on the cause of failure. She has no time for those who complain or get tired, and as far as children go, her special affection is for old heads on young shoulders   youngsters who know where they are going and how they must act to get there.

The wasting of an asset such as youth is to Lucie a crime, and the frugality which she learned in the First World War against her bourgeois background remains a guiding principle. If you are eighty-five you cannot look forward to a long career ahead, but there is still a great deal to be done: a tenth symphony to write, and with determination Lucie maintains her physical fitness and gently tailors her life pattern to allow in the circumstances for the maximum output of work. Even if she never made another pot her output would guarantee her a major place in the history of ceramics as an individual artist of the twentieth century, but she likes to have a target to work to. Early in 1987 she made the permanent trophy for the BBC 'Best Television Designer' award, and the prospect of an exhibition concentrates her mind. As this book enters the final stages of preparation, Lucie has accepted an invitation from the British Council in Vienna to stage an exhibition in the city of her birth. A certain ambivalence in her attitude to Vienna since she left the city made this a difficult decision for her to take, but a historic one. Assembling the pots from private collections is easy enough, but Lucie will always want to be represented by her latest work and some of what she shows in Vienna will have been made over sixty years after the same hands made the first pottery she exhibited there.

The most sensitive of writers about Lucie Rie and her work, George Wingfield Digby, urges in his essay of 1967 that a Lucie Rie pot should be handled. 'The transformation of rock, clay, water and fire can be felt within the finished piece'. When he wrote, Lucie was in mid-career, but he arrives at the essence of Lucie's work then and now. It is not that the act of holding her pot, like a crystal ball, will bring visions of majestic forces. Rather it is that one will appreciate the unity and stillness she achieves by the fusion of glaze and body.

Lucie makes pots, and nothing else. They are vessels, either shallow or tall, abstract and self-justifying. In a sense this makes a creative life more easy – one can go on and on making pots, like chair legs, without asking why one is doing it. In another sense it is much more difficult, for to avoid repetitive vegetating, one must always be seeking after something better, and this has been Lucie's aim and her achievement throughout a long life.

Many photographs, especially of the early pots, were taken before the works were sold into private and public collections, and the artist no longer knows their whereabouts. Where a pot is still in the artist's possession this is indicated in the caption by 'LR'. Pots in other private collections and gallery ownership are acknowledged with permission. Only one dimension is given – height or diameter, as appropriate – and in the case of oval bowls, the maximum width.

Earthenware teapot designed and made for Ernst Plischke, Vienna, 1928. Very dark brown glaze. 13 cm high (less cane handle).

Overleaf: 'These were the pots that nobody liked.' Nobody in England, that is, when Lucie showed the earthenware pots which had brought her acclaim and medals in Europe to English potters such as Bernard Leach, William Honey and Staite Murray. All these pots, which range in height from 22 to 8 cm, are still in the artist's possession. The pot far right is unglazed on the outside, and the surface is burnished red clay. c. 1920–38.

Above and right: earthenware pots made in Vienna in the 1930s. The tall vase (c. 22 cm high) has pronounced throwing lines, which Lucie abandoned in her post-war pottery. The pot on the right has a thick pock-marked glaze, a precursor of the volcanic surfaces of her later stoneware.

Hundreds of earthenware button and jewellery designs, both hand made and moulded, and glazed in many different ways, were produced by Lucie and her workforce in the 1940s.

Oval earthenware bowl, thrown and squeezed, tin glazed inside only and decorated with painted lines in iron oxide. c. 20 cm. c. 1947.

*Three milk jugs, white stoneware with
clear glaze inside, and sgraffito lines
through manganese oxide. c. 11 cm–
28 cm, c.1948.*

The earthenware bowl above bears on its unglazed outside the twin
seals LR and HC, shown right, implying that it was thrown by Hans
Coper, glazed by Lucie Rie. The rare seals are the earliest known for
each potter, LR having been designed for Lucie by Stanley North.
26 cm diam., c.1947. Coll. Sir David Attenborough.

Right: the giant lidded stoneware jar which Lucie has retained in her
workshop since she made it in 1949. It represented a breakthrough in
design, and her first experiments with sgraffito decoration. 47 cm high.

Above: flower basket, stoneware with cream coloured glaze and bamboo handle. 22.5 cm diam., c.1949. Coll. George and Nelly Wingfield Digby. Left: bottle of oval form with squeezed neck and lavender coloured glaze. 16.5 cm high, c.1965.

Right: small stoneware bowls with velvety black glaze and white lines. c.1949. Below: large squared-off stoneware bowl with manganese to darken the rim. c.1952.

Left: stoneware flower vase, with incised design and pale copper green glaze over dark body. Unusually, the rim has been trimmed level after the pot was squeezed oval. 25 cm wide, c.1954. Coll. Charmian Young. Above and right: tiny porcelain pots, each 6.5 cm

high. The yellow pot has a uranium oxide glaze, with iron oxide on the rim, c.1958. Coll. J. Pike. Below: porcelain bowl, decorated with perforations emphasized by manganese, which are covered with a white glaze. 14 cm diam., c.1954. Coll. Cyril Frankel.

Left: ceramic stoneware lidded jar, white glaze, 1949. 360 cm high. Coll. Sir David Attenborough.

Below: porcelain bowl with grey-green glaze. c. 23 cm, c.1967.

Above: porcelain vase with sgraffito decoration through manganese. Chocolate brown. 15.5 cm high, c.1959. Coll. Henry Rothschild.

Two porcelain bowls, with yellow uranium oxide glaze. Above: 16.9 cm diam., c.1959. Coll. Charmian Young. Right: 15.5 cm, 1965. Coll. George and Nelly Wingfield Digby.

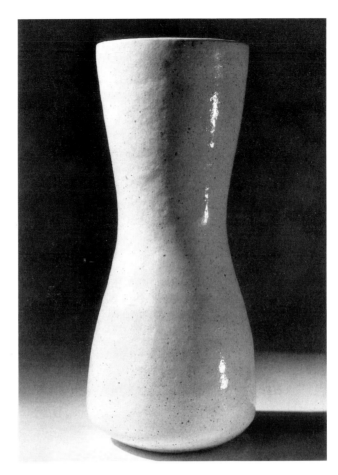

Stoneware vase with white glaze. c. 40 cm high, c.1952. Below: porcelain bowl with grey-green glaze, manganese on rim. c. 250 cm wide, c.1966. Right: black and white vase, 32.5 cm high. Dark areas painted with manganese oxide, light bands bare clay. c.1960.

Metal oxide, inlaid into incised lines in this stoneware pot, has broken through to make black dots, like musical notation, in the words of the owner Charmian Young. 13.8 cm high, c.1959.

Cross hatching into the body of this bowl is inlaid with manganese oxide in the stripe which runs across the inside and the outside of the pot. Manganese is added to the rim. 17.3 cm, c.1962. Coll. Henry Rothschild.

The ferrule of a paintbrush makes the rings
which form the two panels of decoration
on this porcelain vase of squeezed oval
form. 17 cm high, c.1962. Coll. Charmian
Young.

Above and left: porcelain bowls with sgraffito through unglazed manganese band, with creamy white glaze on remaining surfaces, each 14 cm diam. 1951. Top: Coll. City Museum and Art Gallery, Birmingham.

Below: bowl with inlay inside, sgraffito through manganese outside, unglazed. c. 22 cm, c.1972.

Porcelain vase with uranium yellow glaze and sgraffito through manganese. 13.5 cm high, c.1957. Fischer Fine Art.

Below: stoneware bowls with inlaid linear decoration, oval. c.28 cm wide, c.1952.

Heavy porcelain bowl with manganese used for sgraffito and inlaid lines. 26.3 cm wide. This bowl and the blue one on page 111 were made at the same time and bought by Eileen Young from Primavera in 1956.

*Above: bowl coated in manganese with sgraffito
and pink inlay on unglazed rim. c. 16 cm, c.1954.
Below: stoneware platter and porcelain bowl with
sgraffito lines. c.1952.*

*Above: small porcelain bottles varying in height
from 5 to 10 cm, with broad manganese bands and
inlaid and sgraffito design through slip in brown
and blue. 1956–60. Larger pot Coll. Bridget
Appleby; all others LR. Right: porcelain lidded
cigarette box with sgraffito design reminiscent
of a thick bamboo cane. 9 cm high, 1956.
Coll. Robin Tanner.*

Below: hyacinth bowl, felspathic glaze, with streaks bleeding through from the body clay. 19 cm diam., c.1960. Coll. Charmian Young.

Right above: porcelain bowl with bronze rim bleeding mauve into white glaze. 20 cm diam., 1986. Peter Dingley Gallery. Right below: porcelain bowl. 23 cm diam., 1956. Coll. Charmian Young. (See p.107)

Right: black stoneware flower vase showing throwing lines through sgraffito. Inside the main shape is a secondary vase with a narrower neck to hold the stems of the flowers together. This practical pot comes from the same period as the vase on page 94. 19.8 cm high, c.1954. Below: flower vase with asymmetrical top, dry black glaze inside, shining white glaze outside. 13.5 cm high, c.1960. Coll. Charmian Young.

Vase coated in manganese with unglazed white bands. 20 cm high, 1959. Coll. J.W.N. van Achterburgh.

A selection of the familiar chocolate-brown tableware with sgraffito design made in the 1950s.

Milk jug which bears the seal of Lucie Rie made in the 1950s. The potter thinks the handle was made by Hans Coper. Coll. Kristl and Michael Lethbridge.

116

Left above: porcelain goblet with inlaid and sgraffito decoration using manganese. 8.5 cm high, c.1956. Coll. Charmian Young. Left below: porcelain bowl with sgraffito lines through dark manganese band. 15 cm diam., c.1956. Coll. Barbara Gomperts.

Above: unglazed porcelain bowls with sgraffito through manganese inside, and manganese inlay outside. 90–130 cm wide. The more flared bowl on the left was made c.1980, whilst the other three are much earlier, c.1960. Fischer Fine Art. Right: porcelain cigarette box with inlaid lines and a heavy manganese coating. 10.5 cm high, c.1965.

The pot above left with spiralling sgraffito and a central well
has a painted blue band. 15.2
cm, 1961. The glazed pot above
and right has spiralling inlay
and dates from 1959. 21 cm.
Coll. George and Nelly Wingfield Digby. The later bowl,
left, has a thicker coating of
manganese and a much smaller
foot. 20 cm, c.1980.

All the pots on these two pages were exhibited at the Berkeley Gallery in 1960. They range in height from 9 to 20 cm, and all are stoneware with the exception of the black beaker fourth from the left, which is porcelain with a sgraffito leaf pattern. Prices ranged from £2.10s.0d to £6.0s.0d.

Stoneware flower vases, each made in two pieces and squeezed oval. Felspathic glaze over a dark clay containing manganese. 1964. Rear pot 38.2 cm, LR; front pot 34 cm, whereabouts unknown.

122

Stoneware bowl with volcanic surface from silicon carbide. 23 cm, c.1970. Coll. Cyril Frankel.

A family of stoneware pots made in the mid 1960s.

Lucie took the stylized leaf design on this stoneware bowl from a Roman stone bathtub. It was to feature in many of the pots she made in the late 1950s. Here the leaves are blue, the background greenish brown. 28.5 cm diam., 1958. Coll. J.W.N. van Achterburgh.

Right: an early example of the form with incurved top, which Lucie was to make many times from the early 1960s and later called her 'potato'. Some are flattened, this one is left round. 20 cm high, c.1960. Coll. Barbara Gomperts.

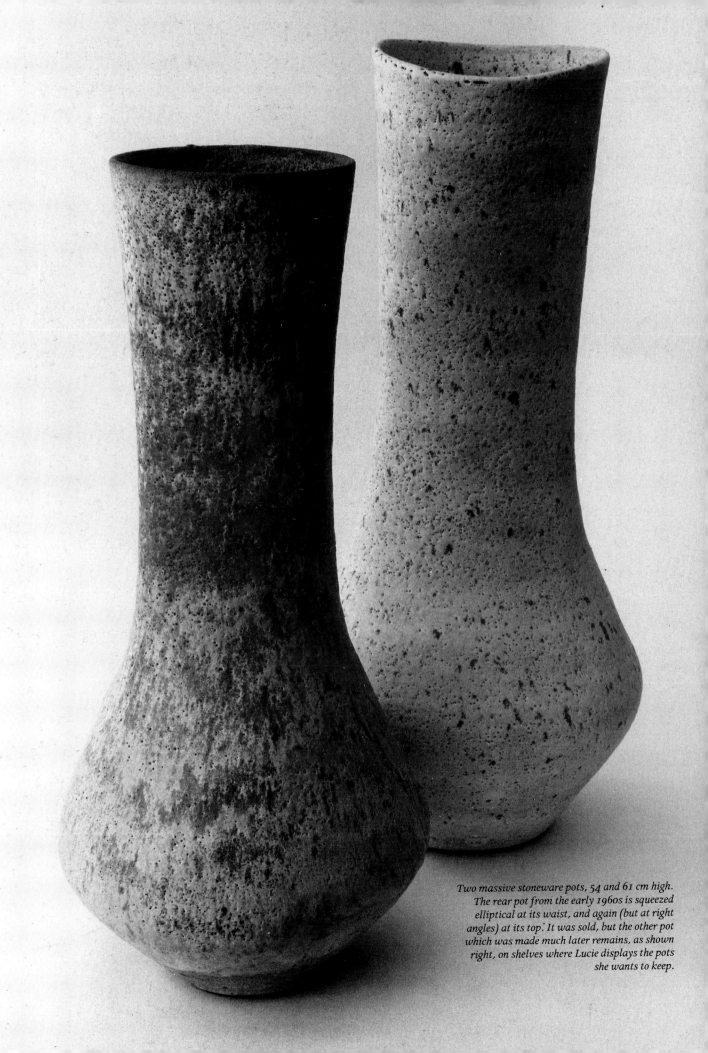

Two massive stoneware pots, 54 and 61 cm high.
The rear pot from the early 1960s is squeezed
elliptical at its waist, and again (but at right
angles) at its top. It was sold, but the other pot
which was made much later remains, as shown
right, on shelves where Lucie displays the pots
she wants to keep.

Oval stoneware bowl bought by the Boymans Museum in Rotterdam for its permanent collection from the 1967 exhibition (see pages 52–3). 25 cm, 1966.

One of the most famous of all Lucie's pots is the massive stoneware platter with unglazed central ring, which has been in the collection of Henry Rothschild for over twenty-five years. Part of the cusped interior of this pot is shown right. 38 cm diam., c.1962.

Left: an incised diagonal pattern shows through the thick glaze of this stoneware pot. c.16cm, c.1965. Below and right: vigorous fluting on three stoneware pots made for the 1960 exhibition at the Berkeley Gallery in London. All pots have a white felspathic glaze over grey.

Smooth and lustrous glaze on stoneware vase. 18.5 cm high, c.1970. Fischer Fine Art.

Viscous felspathic glaze over dark body containing cobalt on a characteristic pot of the 1960s. 12.5 cm high. Fischer Fine Art.

Left: black manganese and tin glaze teapot and accessories from the mid 1950s. The white teapot below is one of the few teapots not to be stained inside with tealeaves, for it has been kept unused in Lucie's workshop as a prototype. 19 cm diam., c.1968. LR.

Below: a classic casserole from the 1960s, with manganese spotting through the tin glaze on dark clay. The unglazed surfaces which touch between lid and lip are lightly stained with manganese. The ring on the top of the knob is wiped clean of glaze. Coll. Dora Raeburn.

Above: three salad bowls with manganese bleeding through tin glaze. Oval, 18 cm wide, c.1956. Fischer Fine Art. Left: sauce-boat, tin glaze with manganese. 14 cm wide, c.1960. Coll. Cyril Frankel.

Right: this large teapot was commissioned by the architect John Pike 'to be big enough for eight cups', and was made about 1965. 17.5 cm high (less handle).

Left: a forest of pots from the 1960s, ranging in height from 17 to over 30 cm. All are porcelain and have bare clay bands on the necks and shoulders, and sgraffito decoration through oxides painted inside the flaring rims and on the necks in brown, blue, red and grey, contrasting with the black manganese sides.

Below: fine sgraffito white on white, on the outside of a bowl which was exhibited in the Arts Council Exhibition of 1967. c. 18.5 cm diam.

Below: large porcelain bowl, 34 cm diam., with inlaid lines through a white glaze in the central area. 1962. Coll. Janet Leach.

Right: two pots taken from the permanent collection of the Boymans Museum in Rotterdam. Left pot, 35 cm high. 1960. The pot on the right is bronze both inside and outside, 20.5 cm high. 1977.

A family of composite pots from the mid 1950s, up to 30 cm high. The three with bulbous centres were made by placing two thrown bowls rim to rim to make a discus-like shape, often with detailed decoration on the opposing flat faces. Those familiar with these pots will know how intricate is the decoration which lies beneath the hollow foot.

Three small stoneware pots, 6 to 7 cm high, c.1970, with spiral decoration from using unmixed clays, cream and green and brown. These pots, the bowls above and the porcelain bowl right, 20.5 cm diam., 1979, are all in the artist's collection.

Three harmonious stoneware pots of the 1960s. The one above has a smooth, flecked glaze like the shell of a bird's egg. 9 cm high. Coll. Kristl and Michael Lethbridge. Below and on the right, the deeply pitted surface shows the effect of Chesterfield red clay in a 'T' material body. The pot below is greenish-brown, 11.5 cm diam. The one on the right, 16 cm high, has a white felspathic glaze coloured by metal oxides breaking through, and both are unglazed towards the foot.

Left: porcelain bottle with sgraffito lines through manganese. 22.5 cm high, 1968. LR.

Above: porcelain bowl with uranium yellow glaze. 11.5 cm diam., 1962. Coll. Henry Rothschild.

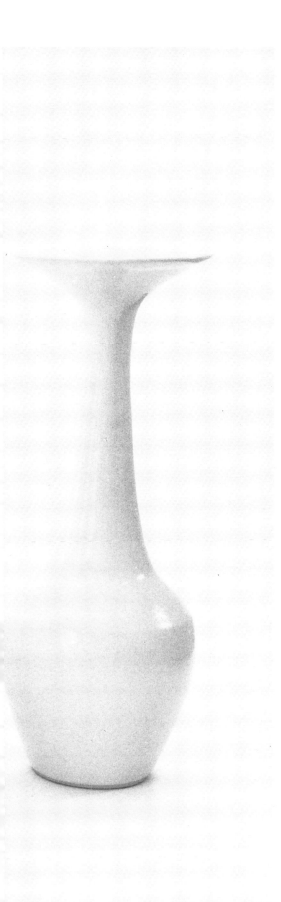

Small porcelain vase, c. 14 cm high, c.1966.

Left: group of porcelain bottles, each thrown in three sections and each undecorated except for a glaze to accentuate the subtle form. From 23 to 35 cm high.

Porcelain pot squeezed oval, glazed with yellow
uranium glaze and manganese rim. 13 cm high,
1960. Coll. George and Nelly Wingfield Digby.

Right: porcelain bowl, 24 cm diam., 1969.
Coll. Henry Rothschild.

Sgraffito is to be found on all the porcelain bowls illustrated which date from the mid 1960s to the mid 1970s.

'This is the colour I cannot get any more' is Lucie's comment about the stoneware bowl, below. The dolomite she used in the glaze is no longer available, so the pots with this dusky pink glaze are rather rare. 22.5 cm diam., 1965. Coll. Dora Raeburn. Right: an even rarer pot, made in the 1970s, with a dark blue body and squeezed oval. 24 cm. Fischer Fine Art.

Celestial stoneware bowls. Left: 1950s. Below: 1969 with spiral from unmixed clays. Lower pot: c. 25 cm diam. Fischer Fine Art.

Left: stoneware bottle made in three pieces. 38 cm high, c.1972, Fischer Fine Art. Above: mirror-black stoneware bowl, 23 cm diam, *c.1960. Coll. Sir Robert and Lady Sainsbury. Below: light green porcelain bowl, 15 cm, early 1970s. LR.*

Left: flat-sided stoneware bottle. 14 cm high. c.1965. Coll. Jane Coper. Below: stoneware bowl with white glaze over dark blue clay. 28 cm diam., 1982. Right: composite vase, spiral pattern darkened with copper oxide. 32 cm high, 1981. Both LR.

Above: black and white porcelain bowl, 25 cm diam., c.1962. Right: pink porcelain bowl with inlay and bronze bands top and bottom from manganese with copper carbonate. 24 cm diam., 1976. LR.

185

186   *Oval vase, lightly crackled felspathic glaze, 18 cm high, c.1979. Coll. Sir Robert and Lady Sainsbury.*

Lava-like glaze with craters from silicon
carbide on massive stoneware bowl.
31 cm diam., 1985. Fischer Fine Art.

'Goitre' pots from the 1980s. Left: white glaze, 32 cm high, 1984, LR. Centre: pale grey, 39.5 cm high, 1984, Fischer Fine Art. Right: a cupboard at Albion Mews. Goitre pot 2nd left, cream, 30 cm, 1980. The centre pot of the three composite vases, right, was illustrated on the commemorative postage stamp issued in October 1987.

Left: composite vase, 35.5 cm, 1980. Coll. Bridget Appleby.
Below: stoneware bowl squeezed oval, c. 32 cm diam., 1986.
Fischer Fine Art.

Above: porcelain vase with red iron oxide and white sgraffito band at the rim. 19 cm high, c.1966, LR.

Right: porcelain bottle with iron slip painted on the inside of the rim and the shoulder, bronze from manganese and copper carbonate. 23 cm high, 1985. LR.

An early example of a favoured shape of the 1960s, thinly coated with manganese. 16 cm high. LR.

Left: large stoneware pots from the early 1960s. Above: distinguished pots from different periods, kept on shelves in the workshop.

196

Three bronze porcelain pots from the 1980s. Left above:
'potato', 8 cm high, LR. Left below: bowl, 16 cm diam.,
Fischer Fine Art. Below: bowl, 21.5 cm. Coll. Jane Coper.
The bronze comes from a coating of manganese and
copper carbonate in the proportions 4:1.

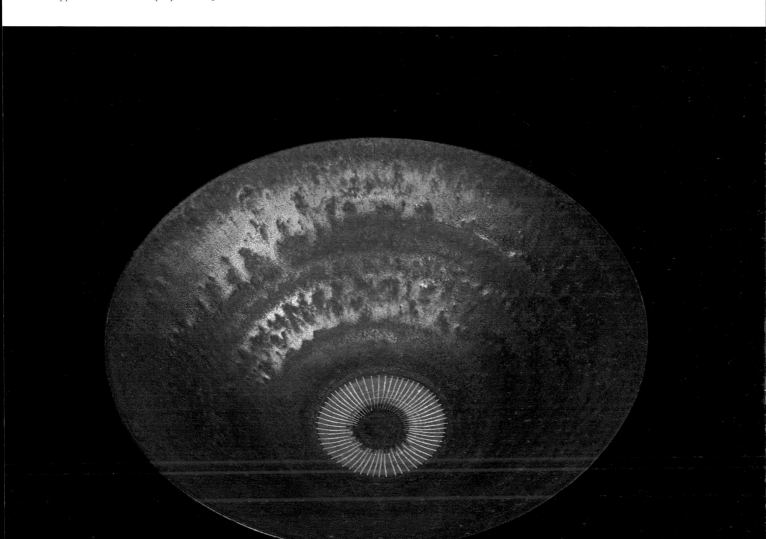

Left: squared-off porcelain bottle thrown in two pieces. 22.5 cm high, 1976. Sainsbury Centre for Visual Arts. Below: porcelain bowl, late 1960s, whereabouts unknown.

Below: porcelain bowl, 23 cm diam., made for Sir Robert Sainsbury in 1983. Right above and below: porcelain pots, manganese bleeding into smooth white glaze. 12 cm and 18 cm diam., early 1980s. Upper, LR. Lower, Fischer Fine Art.

202

Lucie made a small number of composite pots in this form
in the 1970s. Porcelain, sgraffito. 17 cm high. LR.

Above left: composite bottle, black with pink inlay in the inside of the rim. 23 cm high, 1956. Above right: bronze-black bottle, with sgraffito. 24 cm high, 1979. Both LR.

Right: bronze porcelain bowl with mauve inlaid line. 23 cm diam., 1984. Fischer Fine Art

Above: cache-pot *designed for Lady Sainsbury in dark stoneware clay, with grey felspathic glaze. 20 cm high, c. 1975. Right: photographed in the workshop, a pile of knitted bowls and, above, a magnificent and unique shallow bowl with spiral design, thickly glazed, white over grey. 32.5 cm wide, 1981.*

Left: porcelain bottle with pattern under white glaze, 23 cm high.
Above: 'knitted' bowl, 18 cm diam. Both early 1980s, Fischer Fine Art.

Three 'knitted' stoneware bowls. The upper bowls are shown in profile and from above. The one on the right was the first of its kind, 320 cm diam., c.1975. Coll. Jane Coper. Left and above: 19.5 cm diam., 1984. Coll. Dr Max Mayer. Below: 240 cm, 1986. Peter Dingley Gallery.

Above: porcelain bowl with inlaid lines and bronze
bands. 18 cm diam., c.1978. Coll. Jane Coper.

Right: unglazed fine porcelain bowl with cobalt inlaid
lines and manganese bands. 23 cm wide, c.1980.
Coll. Sir David Attenborough.

213

Two stoneware pots of the late 1970s, with similar white glaze. Bottle left: 36 cm high. Right: 16 cm high, LR.

Left: a porcelain pot of a long-favoured design, made in 1986. 19 cm high. Peter Dingley Gallery. Right: porcelain bowl. 23 cm wide, 1987. LR.

The set of seven earthenware jugs shown right, were the first pots ever made in the studio at Albion Mews, and they are still there on display. In front of them is a cream-glazed stoneware vase, 34 cm high, c.1968.

Left: Bronze porcelain vase, 25.5 cm, c.1974. Coll. A. Egner.

'Spinach' bowls made in stoneware with very thick glaze, cratered with silicon carbide. 21, 18 and 15.5 cm wide, 1986. Fischer Fine Art.

221

Chronology

Poppy-head pot, porcelain, 14 cm, c.1970. Coll. Jane Coper.

Note Not all mixed exhibitions to which Lucie Rie has contributed are included.

1902 Lucie Gomperz born in Vienna, 16 March.
1908 Family moves to Falkstrasse, Vienna.
1922 Enters Kunstgewerbeschule as student of Michael Powolny.
1923 First pots exhibited in the Palais Stoclet, Brussels.
1925 Paris, international exhibition.
1926 June: leaves Kunstgewerbeschule with diploma. September: marries Hans Rie.
1928 Moves to apartment at 24 Wollzeile.
1930 Participates in Monza international exhibition.
1934 Work exhibited in exhibition of Austrian art, London.
1935 Gold medallist at Brussels international exhibition.
1936 Gold medallist at Milan Triennale.
1937 Silver medallist at Paris international exhibition.
1938 September: arrives in England.
1939 Moves to Albion Mews.
1940 Marriage to Hans Rie dissolved.
1945 Reopens pottery and button-making workshop after wartime closure.
1946 Hans Coper joins workforce at Albion Mews.
1949 December: first exhibition at the Berkeley Gallery, London.
1950 Berkeley Gallery, shared exhibition with Hans Coper.
1951 Exhibits at Milan Triennale.
    Exhibits in British Pavilion, Festival of Britain.
    December: Berkeley Gallery, shared exhibition with Hans Coper.
1952 July: attends Dartington conference; exhibits in Pottery and Textiles exhibition at Dartington and Edinburgh.
1953 Participates in Engelse Ceramiek exhibition, Amsterdam.
    June: Berkeley Gallery, shared exhibition with Hans Coper.
1954 Exhibits at Milan Triennale.
    New York – solus exhibition at Bonniers Gallery.
    Visits New York and New England.
    Participates in Midland Group exhibition, Nottingham.
1955 Gothenburg – Röhsska Konstslojdmuseet, shared exhibition with Hans Coper.
    September: participates in Midland Group exhibition, Nottingham.

1956 October: Berkeley Gallery, shared exhibition
with Hans Coper.
1957 Minneapolis, University of Minnesota, shared
exhibition with Hans Coper.
1958/9 Participates in touring exhibition, British
Artist Craftsmen, in United States.
1960 June: solus exhibition at Berkeley Gallery.
September: starts teaching at Camberwell School
of Art.
November: participates in Engelse Pottenbakken
exhibition at Boymans Museum, Rotterdam.
1964 Participates in international ceramics exhibition,
Tokyo.
Gold medallist in international exhibition,
Munich.
November: participates in Midland Group
exhibition, Nottingham.
1965 December: Molton Gallery, London, participates
in the Potters' World exhibition.
1966 March: participates in Modern European Pottery
exhibition, John Sparks Gallery, London.
June: solus exhibition, Berkeley Gallery.
1967 April: shared exhibition with Hans Coper at the
Boymans Museum, Rotterdam, and later at the
Gemeentemuseum, Arnhem.
July: retrospective exhibition at the Arts Council
Gallery, St James's Square. Later at Nottingham
and Bristol.
1968 Awarded OBE.
Participates in mixed exhibition at Qantas
Gallery.
1969 Awarded honorary doctorate by the Royal
College of Art, London.
1970 Participates in exhibition in Copenhagen, Osaka,
Kyoto, and at Marjorie Parr Gallery, London.
1971 Participates in first of several annual exhibitions
at Kettle's Yard, Cambridge, organised by Henry
Rothschild.
March: participates in Midland Group
exhibition, Nottingham.
Exhibits at Bradford Museum, Yorkshire.
August: joint exhibition with Hans Coper at
Museum für Kunste und Gewerbe, Hamburg.
Gives up teaching at Camberwell School of Art.
1973 Participates in The Craftsman's Art exhibition at
the Victoria & Albert Museum, London.
1974 Exhibits at Hetjens Museum, Dusseldorf.
1978 April: exhibits at Kunstkammer Köster,
Mönchengladbach.

1979 Bernard Leach dies, Cornwall.
December: solus exhibition at Hetjens Museum,
Dusseldorf.
1981 Awarded CBE.
June: Hans Coper dies, Somerset.
Retrospective exhibition at Sainsbury Centre for
Visual Arts, Norwich, later at Victoria & Albert
Museum, London.
1982 BBC Television 'Omnibus' film with David
Attenborough.
1983 November: solus exhibition at Peter Dingley
Gallery, Stratford upon Avon.
1984 July: shared exhibition with work of Hans
Coper, Fischer Gallery, London.
1986 September: participates in Nine Potters
exhibition, Fischer Gallery, London.
1987 Produces Best Television Designer award trophy
for BBC.
October: participates in exhibition at Fischer
Gallery, coinciding with issue of Post Office
commemorative stamps series 'British Potters'.

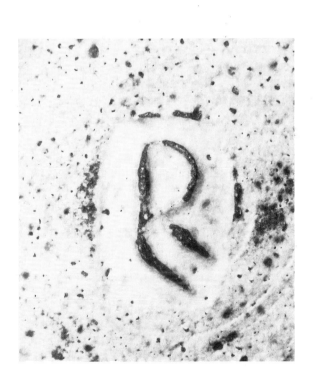

Bibliography

Billington, Dora, 'The Younger English Potters' in *The Studio* March 1953

Birks, Tony *Art of the Modern Potter* London & New York 1967, 1976

—— *Hans Coper* London & New York 1983

Casson, Michael *Potters in Britain Today* London 1967

Clark, Kenneth *The Manual of Pottery* London 1983

Davenport, Tarby, 'The Pottery of Lucie Rie' in *Design* No. 226, October 1967

Digby, George Wingfield *The Work of the Modern Potter* 1951

—— *Lucie Rie* Arts Council exhibition catalogue 1967

Houston, John (Ed) *Lucie Rie* London 1981

Kallir, Jane *Viennese Design and the Wiener Werkstätte* New York & London 1986

Leach, Bernard *A Potter's Book* London 1940

Lewenstein, E. and E. Cooper *New Ceramics* London & New York 1974

Lucie-Smith, Edward *World of the Makers* London & New York 1975

Plischke, Ernst Anton *On the Human Aspect in Modern Architecture* Vienna & Munich 1969

Rose, Muriel *Artist Potters in England* London 1955, 1970

Rothschild, Henry *Contemporary Pottery from Henry Rothschild's Collection* Bristol 1976

Sewter, A.C. 'Lucie Rie – a potter' in *Apollo* February 1954

John Sparks Ltd *An Exhibition of Modern European Pottery* catalogue of the exhibition, 1966

Spielmann, Heinz *Lucie Rie – Hans Coper Keramik*, biographical notes in catalogue of the exhibition, Museum für Kunste und Gewerbe, Hamburg 1972

Picture credits